CLEANLINESS

IN ISLAM

ISLAM IN PRACTICE

A Comprehensive Guide to Tahara

CLEANLINESS
IN ISLAM

Remzi Kuşçular

Light

New Jersey

Published by The Light, Inc.
26 Worlds Fair Dr. Unit C
Somerset, New Jersey, 08873, USA

www.thelightpublishing.com

Library of Congress Cataloging-in-Publication Data

Kusçular, Remzi.
  [Her yönüyle temizlik. English]
  Cleanliness in Islam : a comprehensive guide to tahara / Remzi Kusçular ;
  translated by Süleyman Basaran. -- 1st English ed.
     p. cm.
  Originally published in Turkish as Her Yönüyle Temizlik in 2006.
  Includes bibliographical references and index.
  ISBN 978-1-59784-120-7 (pbk. : alk. paper)
  1. Purity, Ritual--Islam. 2. Islam--Rituals. I. Title.
  BP184.4.K87 2007
  297.3'8--dc22
                                    2007013855

Printed by
Çağlayan A.Ş., Izmir - Turkey
May 2007

TABLE OF CONTENTS

Preface ix

Chapter 1: What Is Cleanliness? 1

What is cleanliness? 3

How important is cleanliness in Islam? 3

What does "Cleanliness is half of faith" mean? 6

What are the degrees of cleanliness? 7

What ritualistic rules concerning cleanliness can
be found in world civilizations? 9

Are all children born spiritually pure? 11

How important was cleanliness for the Prophet? 13

Are we religious because we are clean or should we
be clean because we are religious? 14

What types of cleanliness are there? 15

It is said that "Cleanliness is a proof of God's Existence."
How can this be explained? 16

How can balance be kept in cleanliness? 18

Some people are too apprehensive about cleanliness.
How can they avoid this problem? 20

Does excess in cleanliness cause health problems? 20

Two examples of hygiene obsession 22

Chapter 2: Things That Are Clean and Those That
Are Not in Islam 25

What is filth and purification from filth? 27

What are the types of filth? 27

What is the amount of heavy filth that impedes
the performance of the prayer? 27

What are the things that constitute heavy filth? 28

What are the things that are accepted as light filth? 29

What is the amount of light filth that impedes
  performing the prayer?...29
Is it permissible to use cologne and perfume?...........................30
What are the things that are accepted as ritualistically clean? 31
Are all marine animals pure?...33
Are pets permissible in Islam? 33
What is the ruling on brushes with pig's bristle?......................37
What is the ruling about wearing make-up, using hair dye,
  henna, hair jell, nail polish, lipstick or hair cream?............38
What is the ruling on tattoos on the body? 39
How can one purify from ritual dirt? 39
What are *istinja* and *istibra*?...44
The good manners of *istinja* and *istibra* 44
Abominable (*makruh*) things about *istinja*..............................45
The greatest blessing in the world 46
What are the types of water that can be used for cleansing?......47

Chapter 3: Physical Cleanliness...49

A. Cleanliness of the Body and Garments 51
The general cleansing of body 51
Cleanliness of the mouth and teeth..53
The importance of ablution for physical cleanliness 55
Gold-plated teeth..56
Cleanliness of the hair, beard, and mustache...........................57
Cleanliness and a good appearance 59
Cleanliness of our private parts..60
Cleanliness during menses and pregnancy................................61
Cleanliness of garments 62
Can one pray in ready-made clothes before washing them? 63
Are the clothes ritually clean after dry-cleaning? 63
What is the ruling on detergents used to clean clothes? 64
What is the ruling on praying in clothes smeared with filth? 65
B. Cleanliness of Food and Drinks...65
General information about cleanliness of food and drinks 65
What is the ruling about animals that are not slaughtered
  in the name of God..67
What is the wisdom behind accepting pork as unlawful?..........68

Margarines 69
Beheading and plucking chickens 70
What are the precautions to be taken for cleanliness
 of meat when slaughtering animals? 71
Is it permissible to eat and drink from vessels and
 utensils of non-Muslims? 73
Is it permissible to accept something offered by a neighbor
 one thinks has earned money unlawfully? 73
C. Cleanliness of the Environment 75
 The scope of cleanliness of the environment 75
  1. Cleanliness of houses and residential areas 76
  2. Cleanliness of public places 77
  3. Cleanliness of roads 79
  4. Providing sufficient clean water 80
  5. Cleanliness of the air 81

Chapter 4: Ritual Purification 83
Purification of the ritualistically impure 85
What are the types of ritual impurity? 85
What is ablution (*wudu'*)? 86
 Purification as a preparation for daily prayers 86
 Ablution as both physical and ritual purification 89
 What are the benefits of performing ablution? 91
 What is the wisdom behind ablution? 93
 What is the reward in the hereafter for ablution? 97
 What are the obligatory acts of ablution? 99
 What is wiping with wet hands? 99
 What are the Sunna acts of ablution? 100
 What are the manners of ablution? 100
 What things nullify ablution? 101
 Does crying nullify ablution? 102
 How is ablution performed? 103
 Why did Abu Hurayra exaggerate his performance of ablution? 104
 What are the types of ablution? 105
 What is the ablution of the excused? 106
 What are the benefits of being in a continuous state of ablution? 107
 How does one wipe indoor boots or bandages? 107

What nullifies the wiping of indoor boots? 108

What is ritual bathing (*ghusl*)?.......................................109

What occasions necessitates ritual bathing? 109

What are the types of ritual bathing?.............................110

What are the obligatory acts of bathing? 112

What are the Sunna and manners of bathing? 112

What are the merits and benefits of bathing? 113

What is the ruling of having cavities filled while
  in a state of ritual impurity?.......................................115

What acts of worship are unlawful for those who are
  in a state of ritual impurity?.......................................115

What is the ruling of delaying bathing while being
  in a state of ritual impurity?.......................................116

What is dry ablution (*tayammum*) 117

How is dry ablution performed? 117

What are the rulings of dry ablution?.............................118

When is dry ablution performed? 119

What are the conditions of dry ablution? 119

What is the Sunna of dry ablution?................................120

What things are acceptable for dry ablution?.................120

What things nullify dry ablution? 121

Menstrual, postnatal, and non-menstrual vaginal bleeding.......121

Chapter 5: Spiritual Cleanliness and Purity....................129

Purity of Heart..131

What is to be understood by "purity of the heart"?.........131

What are the signs of a pure heart? 133

What should be done to attain purity of the heart? 135

Cleanliness of Income and Earnings 138

What are the objectives of income and earnings?...........140

What are the impure and unlawful income sources and earnings? ...142

What are the consequences of unlawful earnings?...........147

Notes 151

Bibliography..161

Index...165

PREFACE

In Islam cleanliness, which has been equated by God's Messenger, upon whom be peace and blessings, to "half of faith," is a comprehensive process having material, spiritual, and ritual aspects. In addition to its meanings pertaining to the material world, cleanliness is related to important spiritual issues, including repentance, feeling that we are always under the surveillance of God, examining and calling ourselves to account, and proper servitude to God. Included in the various connotations of cleanliness are cleanliness of income and earnings, a refinement of the states that are ritualistically accepted as impure, and spiritual purification, which means wiping away the filth of sins in the heart.

Islamic commandments are intended to lead humanity to intellectual and spiritual excellence and purity. The daily prayer (*salat*), which is the pillar of religion, cannot be offered without first undergoing the ritual cleansing which is called *wudu'*. The prayers have characteristics that purify human beings of all their sins. Fasting (*sawm*) cleanses evil thoughts from the soul and causes people to avoid evil deeds and all kinds of uncleanness. The prescribed alms (*zakat*) purify a person's riches. Pilgrimage (*hajj*) cures the illness of arrogance and removes any sense of superiority over other people, making one spotlessly clean just like they were on the day they were born. Staying away from unlawful gains and earnings purifies sustenance. It is impossible for a person's heart to be clean without performing these acts of worship. Therefore, the best indication of a purified heart is doing righteous deeds, eliminating what is bad and evil, and exhorting one another to the truth.

After a general introduction to what cleanliness is in the first chapter of this book, issues such as what is clean and what is not in religion, the ways to become purified of filth, and the cleanliness of water will be discussed in the second chapter. We analyze physical cleanliness under subtitles such as cleanliness of the body and garments, cleanliness of food and drink, and cleanliness of residences in the third chapter. As for the purification of ritually unclean states, issues such as ablution (*wudu'*), bathing (*ghusl*), rubbing hands including forearms and face with dust (*tayammum*), and women's menstrual periods will be scrutinized in the fourth chapter. It is also thought appropriate to examine spiritual cleanliness in the last chapter under two subtitles, namely the purity of heart and the purity or cleanliness of earnings.

Throughout this work we have tried to explore issues related to cleanliness in detail. The reader should be aware that divine revelations and hadiths have been recounted in relation to cleanliness as well as judgments of the major schools of Islamic jurisprudence for the issues covered in this book; the opinion that where there are no canonical rules it is the scholars or committees who are qualified to provide legal opinion on canonical matters (*ijtihad*) that have the last say has been taken on board. May God Almighty reward us for our humble efforts.

Remzi Kuşçular

CHAPTER 1

What Is Cleanliness?

What is Cleanliness?

The main word that is used to indicate cleanliness and cleansing in Islam is *"tahara."* Words derived from this term in the Qur'an and other sources mean both purification with water and other cleansing agents, purifying those things that are ritualistically accepted as unclean, and abstention from sins and things forbidden by religion. It also means beautiful manners and chastity.[1] Together with its derivatives, this term occurs 31 times in the Qur'an.

However, there are other Arabic words that also mean cleanliness. *Nazafat* expresses a higher degree of cleanliness and *zarafat* points to delight and delicacy in purification. *Zakat* is used to talk about purifying what one retains after giving up of a portion of the wealth one possesses, and *tazkiya* is used to mean abstention of the carnal soul from sins.

How Important is Cleanliness in Islam?

One of the most important characteristics of nature when it has been untouched by human hands is that it is clean. Cleansing is a task performed by a number of mechanisms, ranging from black holes to microorganisms that groom or clean. This shows that cleanliness is one of the foremost principles of nature. Crows that bury the dead bodies of other crows, the eyelid that protects and cleans the eye, the wind that cleans the earth and rain that filters the dust of the earth are all agents that work in accordance with this principle. Human nature is also clean. It is interesting to see how important cleanliness is for human beings.

Divine religions have placed great importance on the cleanliness of the body and water. Islam is a belief system that is based on physical and spiritual cleanliness. Since the first revelation, this pure belief system has enlightened the horizons of cleanliness and purification, which humanity still tries to reach.

Cleanliness is one of the basic aspects of Islam. It is accepted as both the foundation of the religion and as half of the faith (*iman*). Therefore, people have continuously been encouraged to pursue cleanliness. In order for a Muslim to gain the pleasure of God, they must be clean. God Almighty says in the Qur'an, *"God loves those who turn to Him in repentance, and He loves those who purify themselves"* (Baqara 2:222; see also Tawba 9:108).

It is also revealed in the Qur'an that cleanliness is not a burden for people. After speaking of ablution (*wudu'*), bathing (*ghusl*), and rubbing hands and face with dust (*tayammum*), God says, *"God does not want to put you in any difficulty, but He wishes to purify you and thus complete His favor on you, so that you may be grateful"* (Maeda 5:6).

Moreover, one of the first decrees in Islam is about cleanliness. In one of the earliest verses revealed to God's Messenger, peace and blessings be upon him, God Almighty decrees, *"And purify your garments"* (Muddaththir 74:4). In this verse the close relationship between physical cleanliness and spiritual cleanliness is implied. This verse has also been interpreted by Islamic scholars as metaphorically saying, "Refrain from sexual weaknesses." Thus, believers are ordered to purify their hearts, souls, bodies, garments, and sense of chastity. Concerning this verse Elmalılı Hamdi Yazır asserts that the word *"siyab"* (garments) can also be taken as "carnal soul/ego" or "heart," and that therefore the verse can be interpreted as saying, "abstain from sin, injustice, and bad manners and thus purify yourself or your heart so that your warnings are effective and that your advice be taken." Nevertheless, he points out that there is no reason not to take the verse literally and that it can easily be interpreted to be discussing cleanliness of garments or physical purification. Therefore, it is possible to take the verse as directly pertaining to the physical purification of both body and garments.[2]

It is clear that refraining from physical filth and purifying the heart from spiritual impurities, such as false beliefs and doctrines, associating partners with God, hypocrisy, and other sins are all Islamic and moralistic tasks that are inherent in humankind. In a verse that points to both physical and spiritual cleanliness God says, *"God loves those who turn to Him in repentance and He loves those who keep themselves pure and clean"* (Baqara 2:222).

Cleansing performed before the beginning of the prayers is accepted as a key to the prayers; that is, it is essential for the prayers. Therefore, a person cannot begin to perform prayers without first performing this kind of cleansing, which is called *wudu'* in Islamic terminology. The verse *"Surely a mosque founded on piety from the very first day is more worthy that you should stand in it; in it are men who love being purified; and God loves those who purify themselves."* (Tawba 9:108) was revealed about the people of Quba in Medina, who attached great importance to cleansing as a preparation for the prayers and hence *wudu'*. The Prophet, after telling the people of Quba in Medina that God had praised them for their cleanliness, asked what they had done to deserve that praise. They said in return that they cleaned themselves by combining wiping with water.[3] Indeed, a believer who exhibits his spiritual purity and cleanliness through *wudu'* earns in return the praise and pleasure of God. The fact that cleansing is a prerequisite for the prayers makes it still more important for believers. A person who prepares for daily prayer should make sure that their garments, their body and the place where they will perform the prayer are all clean. Knowing that cleansing is obligatory before beginning the prayer and that daily prayers are the pillars of the religion, every believer has to be clean. Concerning this fact, God's Messenger said: "Cleanliness is the key to prayer."[4]

What is more, it is written in the Qur'an that God ordered the Prophets Abraham and Ishmael to keep the Ka'ba clean for those who circumambulate, for those who retreat, and those who bow down and prostrate.[5] This is very important, for it ascertains that the places where acts of worship are performed and hence the buildings, houses and whereabouts, must be kept clean.

In traditions concerning cleanliness and purification the Prophet says: "Cleanliness is half of faith,"[6] and "God is pure, He loves purity."[7]

WHAT DOES "CLEANLINESS IS HALF OF FAITH" MEAN?

There is a very well-known saying among Muslims which is frequently cited in books as a tradition: "Cleanliness is from Faith." The meaning of this saying is correct; however, such a saying was not directly reported from the Prophet, peace and blessings be upon him. That is, it is possible that it is not an authenticated hadith. Nevertheless, it is true in meaning, since God's Messenger was reported to have said: "*Thuhur* is half of faith, and *al-hamdu lillah* (Praise be to God) fills the scales."[8] The term *'thuhur'* in the hadith has a great number of meanings, including physical cleanliness, and spiritual purification that entails repentance, seeking God's forgiveness, imploring to God, feeling God's continuous supervision, examining and calling oneself to account, and good servitude. A Muslim who leads a life guided by these principles will have a sound, purified heart with a firm belief and will choose what is good, do righteous deeds, and strive to make this prevail over the evil.

We also need to examine another aspect of this issue. Cleanliness, while implying the removal of dirt from the hands, feet, hair, beard, etc. and thus becoming clean and purified, also implies that the heart abstains from the filth and grime of bad manners and sins and is thus exalted towards heavens as if it were on wings. By and by, the heart becomes a mirror for God's benefaction and blessing, and maintains its purity. Through such purity and cleanliness half of faith is attained, which indicates the statement by the Prophet in his tradition, "Cleanliness is half of faith."[9] The other half is God's creation of faith in the heart, as it is God Who guides those who strive to purify themselves to the straight path. While striving to become purified so as to offer worship to God, all the filth and impurity in the heart will be erased, and God will kindle the flames of faith in the heart.[10]

Moreover, prudent and wise scholars (those who can see, evaluate, and appreciate events and incidents not only with their eyes, but also with their hearts) have concluded from the literal meaning of Qur'anic verses related to cleanliness that in Islam purity of the heart surpasses everything in importance. For the Prophet's tradition, "Cleanliness is half of faith" does not only mean cleanliness accomplished with water or the removal of dirt. Indeed, how can such cleanliness be half of faith if the heart is not purified? This would be impossible and unacceptable.

WHAT ARE THE DEGREES OF CLEANLINESS?

There are four levels of cleanliness:

The first level: Purification from outer filth and grime.

The second level: Purification of the limbs from sins.

The third level: Purification of the heart from bad attributes.

The fourth level: Purification of privacy (secrecy or mystery) from *masiwa* (that is, purifying the heart from everything but God). This is the highest level of cleanliness and only prophets and the truthful (*siddiq*, the second highest spiritual rank after prophethood) can attain this degree. Cleanliness at each of these four levels is half the faith pertaining to that level.

The most important aim in purifying the heart is to see the magnificence and greatness of God. The knowledge of God does not truly abide in a heart unless everything other than God is removed from the depths of that heart. For the knowledge of God and things other than God cannot be combined in the same heart. God did not create two hearts in a person's chest; we are not able to put the knowledge of God in one heart and that of all else in the other.

One of the foremost aims of human beings is to adorn their heart with beautiful manners and firm belief as prescribed by religion. The heart cannot take in or absorb beautiful manners or firm belief unless it first is purified from their opposites. Unless sins, bad deeds, and false beliefs, which are all outside the circle of religion, are removed from the heart, the other beautiful attributes do not dwell within it or enlighten it. Thus, purification of the heart is half of faith and is a prerequisite for the other half. This clarifies the meaning of the tradition, "Cleanliness is half of faith." Continuing this line of reasoning, purifying the bodily limbs from all the things forbidden by religion is half of the deeds performed by the limbs and is essential for the existence of the remaining deeds to be carried out. Hence, cleanliness is half of the good deeds that should be performed by one's limbs.

This kind of purification is also essential to perform acts of worship with devotion. This gradation of cleanliness also points to levels of faith. A servant of God can attain each level of faith by passing through each level of purification that pertains to that level of faith. They cannot purify their heart without first refraining from bad attributes nor can they have beautiful manners without first purifying their heart. Spiritual and moral beauty and the splendor of acts of worship cannot be obtained before the limbs have been cleansed from bad manners. The more glorious and honorable the thing that is desired or wished for, the more difficult it is to attain. It is wrong to think that such spiritual ranks can easily be reached. Those who are imprudent and unwise (those who cannot see with the eyes of their heart) will not see the difference between these levels and will only be able to reach the first level not being able to go beyond this lowest level. They become distracted at this simplest level of cleanliness and spend all their time maintaining personal hygiene, washing garments, cleaning the outer parts of body and searching for clean and abundantly flowing water. They are guided by apprehension and illusions, and they falsely believe that the cleanliness that is ordained by God goes no further than their actions. They do not know much about the biographies of leading Islamic figures and of course do not know that such people dedicated a great deal of time and effort to contemplation and to the purification of their heart.[11]

WHAT RITUALISTIC RULES CONCERNING CLEANLINESS CAN BE FOUND IN WORLD CIVILIZATIONS?

God has commanded people in all ages to follow the Messengers and has purified the religion from distortions and transgression through His Messengers, starting with Adam, the first man and ending with Muhammad, the seal of Messengers: *"And assuredly, We have raised within every community a Messenger (to convey the primordial Message): Worship God alone, and keep away from false deities and powers of evil"* (Nahl 16:35). God has appointed Messengers one after the other with clear commands and proofs of the truth so that people in all ages can reach the objective of being purified and prosperous in both worlds.

The existence of ritual purification and cleanliness can be traced in many communities and societies, as it has always been a significant feature of many civilizations throughout history. Today, there are regulations concerning ritual cleanliness in many religions in different parts of the world. Water in eastern religions, such as those in India and Japan, is important for cleansing and purifying. Physical cleanliness is one of the "Four Affirmations" in Shinto. Accordingly, the adherents of this ancient Japanese faith must take baths, wash their hands, and rinse their mouth often. *"Misogi"* is a Shinto practice involving cleansing in a waterfall or other natural running water. Similarly, morning cleansing with water is a basic obligation among the adherents of many Hindu beliefs, and bathing in rivers, especially the sacred Ganges, according to various Hindu beliefs, is a particularly effective form of ritual cleansing. Many religions and faith systems have a ritual cleansing of the dead before burial.

As for ritual purity in monotheistic religions, Judaism shares considerable parallels with Islam in relation to the purity of food, particularly involving the slaughtering of animals. In addition to similar cleanliness enforced for animal sacrifices, some portion of religious Jews distinguish between ritually clean and unclean meat products.

The essential issues concerning the special treatment of the ritual cleansing of bodily fluids in Judaism have conspicuously striking similarities with ritual cleanliness in Islam. The Torah mentions many cleansing rituals relating to menstruation, childbirth, and marital relations, and the laws concerning ritual purity in regard to sexual relations are still observed by some religious portions in many Jewish communities. According to the laws of *niddah* ("menstruant," often referred to euphemistically as *tahara hamishpacha*, or family purity laws), a woman enters a state of ritual impurity when she is menstruating, and sexual relations are prohibited during this time for the couple. In relation to the time of sexual separation during the menstrual cycle, the Torah states, "Do not come near a woman during her period of uncleanness to uncover her nakedness" (Leviticus 18:19). Further, it also states that, "She shall remain in a state of blood purification [after childbirth] for thirty-three days: she shall not touch any consecrated thing, nor enter the sanctuary until her period of purification is complete" (Leviticus 12:4). As for the ritual purification laws for menstruating women in Judaism, it is also important to note that "most Conservative and Reform Jews do not incorporate this aspect of Judaism into their life; it is mainly Orthodox Jewish families that practice these laws."[12] The cleanliness instructions in the Torah have changed over time into more of a spiritual ritual for menstruating women. The ritual cleanliness of men, on the other hand, is not a significant practice although the impurities which occasion the need for bathing applies to both men and women in Islam.

As a religious requirement of the Muslim and Jewish faiths, both Muslims and Jews practice circumcision for male cleanliness. According to a clear statement in the Bible, Abraham was circumcised as "a sign of the covenant" (Genesis 17:11). Christianity replaced this practice of circumcision with baptism, which is widely practiced in almost all Christian denominations. Like circumcision, baptism is a once-in-a-lifetime event and generally includes immersion, aspersion, or anointment with water. Although male circumcision was strictly prohibited with a bull in 1442 in answer to the Coptic Christians' observance of the practice of circumcision, and ordered "all who glory in the name of Christian not to practice circumcision either before or after baptism,"[13] the practice of male circumcision continues to be optional among Christians. It is still observed among Ethiopian and Coptic Christians, and circumcision rates are also high today in the Philippines and the US.

Ritual purification through the induction of a newborn or of a grown-up into Christianity is through baptism and is widely practiced in almost all Christian denominations. Beyond being a sign of reception into the Church, it is believed that the stain of original sin is removed from the baptized individual.

ARE ALL CHILDREN BORN SPIRITUALLY PURE?

Every child is born in a state of spotless purity and with a natural essence pertinent to faith and Islam as attested in the Qur'an: "*So set your purpose for religion as a human by nature upright – the nature (framed) of God, in which He has created human*" (Rum 30:30). The idea of being guilty of a sin one did not commit is inconceivable in Islam, and an apparently innocent baby is neither born innately sinful nor personally subject to the effects of a sin they never committed. As stated in a Qur'anic verse, "*Every soul earns only to its own account; and no soul, as bearer of burden, bears and is made to bear the burden of another*" (Anam 6:164); nobody can be held responsible for the deeds of someone else. A person is responsible only for the manner in which they have exerted their own will and not the will of other persons as declared in the following Qur'anic verses, "*there is nothing for human but that which he strives for,*" (Najm 53:39) and "*no bearer of burden shall bear the burden of another*" (Zumar 39:7). Thus, no one can be burdened with the burden of another, nor absolved of any crime or sin they have committed through the suffering of another, as attested in another verse:

> And a burdened soul cannot bear the burden of another, and if
> one weighed down by burden should cry for (another to carry)
> his burden, nothing of it shall be carried, even though he be

near of kin. You warn only those who fear their Lord in secret and keep up the prayer; and whoever purifies himself, he purifies himself only for (the good of) his own soul; and to God is the eventual coming. (Fatir 35:18)

These have considerable parallels with the following teachings of the Bible:

The soul who sins is the one who will die. The son will not share the guilt of the father, nor will the father share the guilt of the son. The righteousness of the righteous man will be credited to him, and the wickedness of the wicked will be charged against him. (Ezekiel 18:20)

The fathers shall not be put to death for the children, neither shall the children be put to death for the fathers: every man shall be put to death for his own sin. (Deuteronomy 24:16)

But the children of the murderers he slew not: according unto that which is written in the book of the law of Moses, wherein the Lord commanded, saying, The fathers shall not be put to death for the children, nor the children be put to death for the fathers; but every man shall be put to death for his own sin. (2 Kings 14:6)

Islam entertains no idea of the universal sinfulness of the human race as every new-born child is born in a state of *fitrat* as attested by the Prophet Muhammad: "There is none born but is created to his true nature (*fitrat*)."[14] So, every child is born with a pure nature, no matter whether they are born of Muslim or non-Muslim parents.

At birth, every child is like a spotlessly white piece of paper, a *tabla raza*, dough ready to take any shape, ore awaiting the mold, or a sapling waiting to be shaped. A person diverges and thus becomes alienated from their *fitrat* (inborn natural predisposition) not because of any innate wrong within their nature, but mostly because of the social circumstances they find themselves in. It is the parents who most influence the religion of the child by raising the child with respect to their worldly situation.

The pure and benign predisposition of a child can be stained and dulled with unbelief and sins. With unbelief and a denial of God's existence, human beings close their eyes to the countless proofs that point to God's existence, they plug their ears, drowning out the voice of their heart, dulling and spoiling their predisposition, depriving themselves of sources of light, and losing their way in the dark. On the other hand, with faith and good deeds the same person is able to protect their predisposition, which is originally pure, and maintain its purity. Thus, it is possible to say that the natural disposition of human beings is principally inclined towards faith and that unbelief is only accidental. *Fitrat*, which is initially pure, can later be tainted. If a person does not take precautions to protect the original purity of their *fitrat*, they can easily be carried away by any of the movements of unbelief.

When a person stains and spoils their *fitrat*, they take on a second *fitrat*, which is flawed and impure. Even though a newly-hatched bird cannot fly, it is still a bird. It has an inborn ability to flying. By and by, as it grows up, jumps and tries to fly we say, "This bird will fly." However, if an external element causes the bird to lose its ability to flying, bird or not, it cannot fly. This is the same as unbelief. That is, it is like breaking the wing of a bird and locking it up in a cage; unbelief, too, spoils the original pure *fitrat* of a human being and gives that person a second corrupt one. Seeing a newly born baby we can say, "This is believer" or "This will become a believer" just as we can say that a newly-hatched bird is "a bird." But if that baby is ravaged by the harsh winds of unbelief and if they misuse their willpower while growing up, if they lose the purity of their natural predisposition they become buried under the dark earth of unbelief. They cannot get enough heat, light and rain to flourish and become a blessed tree that bears fruit every season.[15]

HOW IMPORTANT WAS CLEANLINESS FOR THE PROPHET?

The Messenger of God, peace and blessings be upon him, who was adorned with the eloquent manners of the Qur'an, is an example for us with his cleanliness, just as he is with all his other attributes. Throughout his life he paid attention to cleanliness, wore clean and elegant clothes, particularly when going to the mosque or visiting people; he used pleasant scents, and refrained from eating things such as raw onions or garlic, so as not to disturb others. "Keep your surroundings clean,"[16] he said and thus advised us to keep the environment clean. He wanted his community and followers to maintain the cleanliness of public places as well.

We should pay great attention to both physical and spiritual purity, and we should keep our environment and our bodies clean. God's Messenger, peace and blessings be upon him, informed us that cleanliness is half of faith[17] and wanted his companions and followers to cleanse their body at least once a week.[18]

Indeed, God's Messenger gave utmost care to personal hygiene. No matter if it was day or night, he used to wash his mouth and nose,[19] cleanse his teeth and take ablution before going to bed and after getting up.[20] He said that cleansing the teeth would not only maintain oral health but also help us earn God's pleasure[21] and that we should wash our hands whenever we wake up from our sleep.[22] Moreover, he used to dry his face and limbs with a towel after he washed them.[23]

ARE WE RELIGIOUS BECAUSE WE ARE CLEAN OR SHOULD WE BE CLEAN BECAUSE WE ARE RELIGIOUS?

A person can be clean without being religious. There are people who are clean from head to foot and who are admired for their cleanliness. However, it is possible that some of these people do not believe in God. On the other hand, there are religious people who perform daily prayers five times a day, but who are absolutely filthy. Here an important point must be underlined: If a person is faithful and religious, they have to accept that cleanliness is a fundamental principle of the religion. Islam has ordained Muslims to wash themselves (ablution, ritualistic cleansing; not necessarily a complete bath) five times a day before daily prayers. Whereas the Hanafi School of Islamic Jurisprudence accepts the having of a bath once a week as *sunna* (practice of the Prophet, which believers are strongly advised to follow), some schools have ordained it to be obligatory. In any case, having a bath (*ghusl*) every Friday is recognized as *sunna al-mu'akkada*, which is a confirmed practice of the Prophet and which would be sinful to habitually neglect. Indeed, the virtues and merits of Friday, which is the holy day for Muslims, can only be observed after a complete purification of the body.

All these clearly show that cleanliness is very important in Islam. A person has to be clean so as to live up to the principles of Islam. If someone does not adhere to all the Islamic principles but neglects some of them, they are not irreligious. But they will be unable to fully benefit from the bounties and blessings of the religion.

WHAT TYPES OF CLEANLINESS ARE THERE?

In Islamic culture, personal hygiene and ritualistic cleansing complement each other and cannot be thought of as separate entities. Hence, Islamic scholars have classified cleanliness as consisting of physical cleanliness, ritual cleanliness, and spiritual cleanliness.

Physical cleanliness comprises cleanliness of the body, garments, food, drink, and environment. As for spiritual cleanliness, this has broader meanings. This type of cleanliness includes purity of a Muslim's intentions, heart, thoughts, intellect, language, as well as their relationships with other people and their earnings. In its broadest context, it is possible to say that cleanliness or purity of faith is also included in spiritual cleanliness.

Sins are the filth and impurity that reach the heart and they must be cleansed through repentance and a sincere desire for God's forgiveness. There are many sins, such as hypocrisy, lying, and backbiting, which, although not visible, pollute and spoil the morals and intentions of believers. Muslims should purify themselves from these sins by good manners and sincerity in faith and righteous deeds.

The essence of religion is purifying oneself from spiritual filth, knowing God, the exaltation of the soul through obedience and worship to Him and thus having a firm connection and relationship with Him. Physical conditions should also be appropriate for the exaltation of the soul. This is confirmed by the fact that Islam forms a close relationship between worship, spiritual purification, and physical cleanliness, as well as the fact that the Qur'an speaks of cleanliness as a way to both physical and spiritual purification.

Ritualistic cleansing from sins, which is another kind of cleanliness, means taking ablution (*wudu'*) in order to purify oneself from ritual impurity. Getting rid of visible filth and dirt is called "*tahara min najasa,*" and eliminating the state of ritual impurity by taking ablution is called "*tahara min hadath*" in Islamic terminology. Ablution is not an act of worship in itself nor is at an end, but rather is a means that enables Muslims to be allowed to perform worship and helps them become morally and spiritually prepared for the acts of worship so that they can benefit from them in the best possible way. In addition, there are certainly many physical and worldly benefits as well, which will be explained in detail in the following chapters.

It should be emphasized that there is a close relationship between physical and spiritual purification. They cannot be separated from one another. Each of these two types of cleanliness has both physical and spiritual dimensions. In Islam, just as it is mandatory to cleanse a dirty body from its physical dirt, so too, it is essential to purify the soul from sins, which can be seen as spiritual filth and dirt.

IT IS SAID THAT "CLEANLINESS IS A PROOF OF GOD'S EXISTENCE." HOW CAN THIS BE EXPLAINED?

It's better to start answering this question by giving an example. If 999 gates of a palace are open and only one is closed, nobody can argue that the palace cannot be entered. Thus, a person who denies the existence of God, in fact, wants to focus on the one gate that is always closed. Indeed, that gate is closed to the spiritual world of those who are like this person because of the obstacle that is in front of their eyes. There are no closed gates for believers if they do not close their eyes. In any case, 999 of them are wide open for everybody.

Certainly, the proof of cleanliness is one of those gates and proofs. *Nazafat* (pure cleanliness) and cleanliness are inherent in human beings; the earth and the entire universe clearly indicate the One Who is called *"Al-Quddus"* (the Most Holy, the Purest). Bacteria, bugs, ants, and scavengers that clean the earth; wind, rain, and snow; icebergs and fish in the oceans; the atmosphere around the world, black holes in the sky; oxygen that refines the blood in our body and spiritual breezes which save our souls from distress and despair all tell us of God's Name, *"Al-Quddus"* (The Holiest) and prove the existence of the Holy Being.[24]

While the erythrocytes in our blood destroy germs and other harmful elements that enter the body, and thus follow the *Sunnatullah* (God's Law), the air that we inhale and exhale purifies our blood and thus verifies that it is subject to the same Divine Law. Eyelids cleanse the eyes. Flies conform to the same rule when wiping and cleansing their wings. The wind blows the dirt and dust that gathers on earth and purifies it. Clouds sprinkle water on the gardens of the earth like a wet sponge, and settle the dust and dirt on the earth. Then they withdraw, taking with them the dirt they have collected in an orderly manner, as if not to pollute the skies. They wash 'the face' of the earth and the sky, make them spick and span and finally leaving them with a sparkling beauty. All these examples show that the Divine rules concerning cleanliness function perfectly and in an orderly manner. The fact that there is general cleanliness in the universe is a manifestation of God's Name *"Al-Quddus."*

To think that human beings can ignore this general Law of God is not feasible. For, all entities in the universe, from atoms to stars, comply with the law of cleanliness, which is a result of God's name *"Al-Quddus"*. Indeed, God Almighty has subjected human beings, who are the most exalted and vulnerable entity created by Him, and has made them responsible for physical and spiritual cleanliness. Ignoring such a law, followed by all animate and inanimate creatures, and opposing the order of the Ruler of the Heavens and the Earth is certainly a great act of heedlessness and amounts to a revolt against God. It is an atrocity committed against the rights of God and those He created. *"Al-Quddus,"* one of His great names, necessitates cleanliness; for this reason cleanliness is accepted in the Prophet's traditions as being the light and perfection of faith. Also in the Qur'anic verses physical and spiritual cleanliness is depicted as a means of securing and earning God's good pleasure.[25]

How can Balance Be Kept in Cleanliness?

Imbalance in thought of servitude causes some people to say "I have a pure heart" and then neglect acts of worship. There is a group of ignorant people who think in this way and say "my heart is pure, there is no need for worship; reading books and conversation is better than that, worship can be expiated, but these cannot." Certainly, this is making a mockery of religion and a symptom of the illness of excess that exists in society.

While performing worship, some other groups of people pay attention to the details, being sensitive only to structures and forms. For instance, they carry a prayer rug with them as if it is necessary that they put their forehead on the mat but not the ground while performing their prayers. Some others, although not obligatory, wear special clothes for daily prayers and still some others behave strangely when trying to do *istibra* (ensuring the cleanness of undergarments and private parts after relieving oneself). Neither our beloved Prophet nor any of the Islamic scholars did any of these things.

Most probably, those who are excessively interested in their outer appearance are not so sensitive about their inner self, and they are unaware of impurity or stains on their heart. We should realize that, no matter how sensitive a person is about their *istibra* or *wudu*, if they pay no attention to their inner world and disregard the meaning and purpose of the things they do, they will not be rewarded for their actions and they will be turned away, empty-handed in the Hereafter.

Islam is a religion of ease. Those who make it difficult are the ones who do not understand it. God's Messenger says the following: "Religion is very easy and whoever overburdens himself in his religion will not be able to continue in that way."[26] Indeed, religion is something that is lived. It is above and beyond ideas such as neglecting worship, saying that one's heart is pure, or insisting on not putting one's forehead on the ground without a prayer rug. The level of person's servitude to God is as great as their devotion. They must not do additional artificial things to try to show that they have a greater devotion; otherwise they will violate the balance. They will not earn God's pleasure but will be tormented if they do not have an inner integrity and if they are interested only in form or appearance. They must be on guard not to be misled by Satan or to become so self-absorbed that they refuse to put their forehead on the ground; the prophets put their foreheads on the ground, and so must we. To pursue such actions will only bring about an imbalance.

The prophets demonstrated a balance in all acts of worship. People can stay on the right path only if they follow the prophets and perform acts of worship as they instructed. In this context, for instance, water is used to perform ablution. When there is no water, as is declared in the Qur'an, earth or sand can be used for ablution by rubbing the hands and face with dust (*tayammum*) instead of water and then praying. However, a Muslim must also pay attention to inner purity and enlightenment. For, a complete cleanliness can only be attained in this way and this is the most beautiful way of preparing for acts of worship. Believers must purify themselves as ordained by religion and take great care so as not to let even a drop of urine splash on their body or garments. When they do *istibra*, they do it in the most appropriate place and wait for the release of urine to cease as it is compulsory that they ensure the drops of urine have come to an end. Whenever they enter the toilet with their left foot first they say, "O Lord! I take refuge in You from Satan who is filthy, who was dismissed from Your presence and Your benevolence."[27] Thus a person promises to beware of any dirt that they may come into contact with. Hence, people remind their carnal souls (*nafs*) of purity and take refuge in God from spiritual impurity. When a person has relieved themselves, they leave the toilet and say: "All praise be to God Who removes from me what is harmful and makes me healthy."[28] Those who are unable to relieve themselves of their urine can tell us what a great relief it is to be able to do so.

SOME PEOPLE ARE TOO APPREHENSIVE ABOUT CLEANLINESS. HOW CAN THEY AVOID THIS PROBLEM?

Apprehension or misgiving is the last resort Satan uses to attack believers. Those who have newly begun to be sensitive about worship have no misgivings. Rather, people who are deeply devoted to religion usually feel apprehensive. Satan can cause apprehension and introduce doubts in matters of faith.

When a believer thinks deeply about a worry and sees it as a problem, it can become an illness. In this case, the believer should seek professional help. If a believer is doubtful about whether or not they have wiped their head while performing ablution or whether or not they washed one of their limbs, they should say, "I washed it" and go on to perform the prayer. This is better, even if they did not actually wash it. When they are doubtful about whether they have performed three or four *rakats*, and if they frequently have such doubts, then they should accept that they have performed four *rakats*. This solution will help to eliminate apprehension. The believer should face and counter-attack those things that are being inflicted on them by their carnal soul (*nafs*) and the best way to do this is to simply ignore these apprehensions and do the opposite of what the apprehension calls you to do. For, Satan's purpose in this is to make acts of worship difficult for the believer and make them abandon them all together.[29]

DOES EXCESS IN CLEANLINESS CAUSE HEALTH PROBLEMS?

It may seem to many people that there can be no excess in or apprehension about cleanliness. However, there are people that have such problems. Obsession with or anxiety about cleanliness can cause great harm to an individual. Studies show that those who overprotect themselves from dirt and germs while growing up are more likely to get asthma and other allergic ailments.

Air pollution was thought to be one of the causes of asthma. Asthma attacks are ignited by particles in the lung which start a false defensive reaction. But this does not mean that more air pollution causes more particles or more serious asthma. For instance, although Poland has heavily polluted cities, asthma and other allergic ailments are less prevalent there than in southern Sweden, where the air is relatively clean. According to David Strachan, an epidemiologist[30] at London School of Hygiene and Tropical Medicine, children that have several elder sisters or brothers, that is, those who come from large families are often immunized against hay fever, childhood eczema, and asthma. Strachan claims that the dirt and germs the older siblings carry into the home also bring with them many infections and this protects the younger siblings against allergies.

Asthma specialist Thomas Platts Mills from Virginia University, Charlottesville reports that children living in cities in Central America get many infections early in their life but that there is no high or extraordinary risk of asthma. Strachan, too, asserts that studies conducted on human beings show that earlier infections prevent future allergies.

Nowadays, proponents of the hygiene hypothesis try to explain the mechanism in which too much hygiene may harm the immune system of the human body. Their next objective is to define what kind of hygiene is harmful to the immune system.

Childhood infections are only one part of the story. Various germs which live in the human body also have a certain role in this. John Stanford Hook, a bacteriologist[31] at London College, says that pollution has a very specific bacterial content and that this protects people who are not overly clean from getting asthma, hay fever, and other allergies.

In urbanized communities, people spend little time in the open air and come into contact with very little dirt. This considerably lowers their chance of being infected by bacteria. Less frequent contact with bacteria can explain this high number of asthma cases. Few people who live in large cities have houses with gardens. They tend to detach their houses from the environment and adopt an overly-hygienic way of life. However, the human immune system needs this outside world. If we are not in touch with a sufficient number of bacteria and viruses in our life, we may later have to have them introduced into the system through vaccination. While partly protecting us, too much hygiene deprives us of some other things and induces a great cost in health. We now realize that extreme hygiene causes some autoimmune ailments[32] and allergies. Water that is partially muddy has no economic value but provides the immune system of the body with a chance to flex its muscles.

Two recent studies indicate that it is possible to develop vaccines to prevent asthma and other allergies and to empower the immune system. Julian Hopkins of Oxford University has tested a "mycobacterium vaccae" vaccine and is hopeful that he may find a remedy for these ailments. If proponents of the hygiene hypothesis are justified in their claims, new vaccines should be developed and the present ones should be reviewed. More importantly, urbanized communities that are obsessed with hygiene will have to re-evaluate their distaste and fear of microorganisms.[33]

TWO EXAMPLES OF HYGIENE OBSESSION

Howard Hughes was a wealthy American who had a peculiar habit. He died a recluse in 1976. This man had not spoken face to face with anyone for years out of the fear that they might be "carrying an illness." This microbe-phobia caused him to pass his final days in a hotel in Beverley Hills living alone. He spent most of his time wrapping his belongings in napkins in this room, for which he was paying millions of dollars.

Sheikh Abu Said, who lived during the reign of Sultan Suleyman the Magnificent, had a similar illness. He used to have nine baths a day. He would never touch anybody and would never let anybody touch him. When Vizier Samiz Ali Pasha told Sultan Suleyman about the Sheikh, the Sultan wanted him to be brought to his presence. The Vizier answered: "Your Majesty, he will not come. For, if he comes, he will have to go on his knees and kiss Your Majesty's dress. So, he will not do this." The Sultan abrogated all the protocol so that he could see the Sheikh. When the Sheikh came into his presence, the Sultan said: "May God be pleased with you, for you enlighten the youth with your knowledge." Then he turned to the vizier and asked: "What is the Sheikh's wage?" Learning that it was one hundred silver coins, he said: "One hundred is not enough. Add one hundred more for the soap he uses so that he can purify the sense of doubt and apprehension from his heart." After this incident, the Sheikh abandoned his deep obsession with hygiene.

Obsession with cleanliness can hinder a believer's willingness to perform prayers and thus cause them to forget God. They may even become a laughing-stock for Satan, whose main aim is to make believers neglect acts of worship. Therefore, with the view that excess in anything is wrong, we have to find the moderate way.

CHAPTER 2

Things That Are Clean and Those
That Are Not in Islam

What is Filth and Purification from Filth?

Physical dirt is called *najasa* in Islamic terminology. Something that is impure and filthy is *najis*. Purifying oneself from the *najasa* means purifying the body, garments, and places where the prayers are performed from things like blood, urine and feces of human beings or animals.

While some of these are intrinsically unclean, the impurity of some other things can be caused by external factors. For example, pus is *najis* in itself, but a garment which is essentially clean becomes impure when contaminated by pus.

What are the Types of Filth?

There are two types of actual or ritual filth (*najasa*):

a) Heavy filth (*najasa al-ghaliza*)
b) Light filth (*najasa al-khafifa*)

This classification is not based on the amount of dirt, but on whether or not it harms the validity of daily prayers. For, whether heavy or light, they are equal in their ability to dirty things. For example, if any filth contaminates water, it makes the water filthy and it is not permissible to perform ablution with such water.

What is the Amount of Heavy Filth That Impedes the Performance of the Prayer?

The amount that impedes performance of the prayer depends on whether the filth is dry or not. To put it more clearly, if heavy filth is something dry, it must weigh less than three grams, or 0.106 of an ounce to not have an effect. If it is more than three grams, or 0.106 of an ounce, it needs to be cleansed for the prayer. If it is something wet and if it has dirtied a place wider than the palm of a hand, it is again an impediment for performing the prayer. A believer must purify themselves or their garments from this kind of filth to be able to perform the prayer. Any dirt less than these amounts does not have to be removed for the prayer. Nevertheless, if possible, it should be washed off. This is the best way and the practice of the Prophet, peace and blessings be upon him.

WHAT ARE THE THINGS THAT CONSTITUTE HEAVY FILTH?

Heavy filth is as follows:

- Anything that is evacuated from the human body that necessitates *wudu'* (ablution) or *ghusl* (complete ritual bath): urine, feces, semen, *mazi*,[1] *wadi*,[2] pus, yellowish water, a mouthful of vomit or blood, menstrual and postnatal blood, as well as non-menstrual vaginal bleeding.
- Urine, saliva, and the feces of animals whose meat cannot be eaten. However, feces of some birds whose meat is not permissible to be eaten, such as an eagle or a hawk, is accepted as light filth. Of the animals whose meat cannot be eaten, only a cat's saliva is not ritualistically impure.
- Flowing blood of all animals. However, blood that remains in the edible meat, liver, heart, and spleen is accepted as pure.
- Feces of poultry, like chicken, goose, duck and turkey, whose meat is permissible. However, the feces of animals whose meat is permissible which defecate in the air, like sparrows or pigeons, is accepted as ritualistically pure.
- The carrion of terrestrial animals and those slaughtered without saying "Bismillah" and their non-tanned skins.
  The meat of an animal that is slaughtered by cutting its throat is also accepted as ritualistically impure and cannot be eaten by Muslims if it has not been slaughtered as defined

precisely by religion. The ritual of slaughtering animals mandated by the religion is to say *"Bismillah"* or "in the name of God." If this ritual is deliberately neglected, the meat of the slaughtered animal cannot be eaten. If one forgets to pronounce this, then there is no harm in eating the meat.

- Alcoholic drinks. It is unlawful to consume alcoholic drinks or to perform the prayers if one's body and garments are contaminated by alcohol. These things are accepted as ritualistically filthy.[3]

WHAT ARE THE THINGS THAT ARE ACCEPTED AS LIGHT FILTH?

- Urine and feces of animals whose meat can be eaten.
- The feces of wild birds which defecate in the air and whose meat cannot be eaten. But, the feces of birds like pigeon and sparrow, whose meat is permissible, is ritualistically clean and thus is not an obstacle for daily prayers.

WHAT IS THE AMOUNT OF LIGHT FILTH THAT IMPEDES PERFORMING THE PRAYER?

If one-fourth of the body or garment is contaminated with light filth, this is an obstacle for the prayer and it is obligatory to cleanse the contaminated item. If it is less than this amount, it is not an impediment for performing the prayer. However, even if the filth is less than this amount, it would be more appropriate, according to the principles of Islam, to purify oneself from such light filth. Our beloved Prophet points to the fact that those who take care of cleanliness have a powerful faith when he says: "Cleanliness is half of faith." Therefore, believers should keep their body, garments, and the places where they perform acts of worship as pure and clean as possible. They should clean any dirt, even if it is less than the amount that impedes performing the prayers.[4]

IS IT PERMISSIBLE TO USE COLOGNE AND PERFUME?

Before making any judgment as to whether something is lawful or not, the ingredients of that thing should be checked. If analyses of its contents reveal that it contains something unlawful, then it is prohibited (*haram*). Otherwise, it cannot be considered as unlawful. This principle is also applicable in the case of scents. As cologne and most perfumes contain alcohol, they are accepted as heavy filth (*najasa al-ghaliza*). Although some Hanafi scholars are of a different opinion concerning the use of them, most of them agree that a little amount of something which is unlawful is also unlawful.[5]

However, there is a different aspect to the use of cologne and perfume. They are not used as a beverage, but are used for scent and, in the case of cologne in particular, used against germs. Nevertheless, this should not mislead believers. Just as drinking alcohol is unlawful, it is also not right to perform prayers in clothes that are smeared with alcohol. For, any kind of alcohol is filth of an extreme degree, in the same manner as urine, for the illegality of it has been indisputably proven. Thus, cologne and perfume are accepted as something that are unclean and just as in the case of urine if they make a mark on the body or clothes larger than the palm of one's hand this will invalidate the prayers. Even though some people say that the alcohol evaporates, not all of it disappears. Scientists say that even after evaporation, some part of the alcohol remains on the skin or clothes. If evaporation made such things permissible, then, even the mark of urine would be accepted as something that does not nullify prayers. Certainly, this is not acceptable. Thus, the evaporation and drying out of cologne or perfume through wind, heat, etc. is not sufficient to purify it. It must be washed out.

There are pores on the skin and these absorb liquids. Therefore, such liquids can be absorbed by the skin and this should be avoided. As for the claim that cologne kills germs, there are differing views. According to researchers, cologne does not kill germs, but blocks and prevents their spread. Hence, it is meaningless to insist on using something about which there is no clear information. However, it should be kept in mind that there are some scholars who say, for example, that cologne is permissible when it is difficult to refrain from it. For instance, although it is forbidden to consume any intoxicants, according to two resolutions taken by the Din İşleri Müşavere Kurulu (Religious Affairs Council in Turkey) in 1943 and 1948, it is permissible to use cologne elsewhere or for purposes other than drinking. There is no harm in using alcohol to produce light or heat, or as a chemical substance. The Qur'anic verse that was revealed before alcohol was completely forbidden says that there are some benefits in alcohol: *"They ask you about intoxicants and games of chance. Say: In both of them there is a great sin and means of profit for men, but their sin is greater than their profit..."* (Baqara 2:219). This is the clear explanation of the Qur'an. Indeed, today alcohol is used to produce light and heat.

When using scent, we should take into account the presence and pleasure of pure spirits and angels. According to Prophetic sayings, pure spirits enjoy good odors. That is to say, they are attracted by sweet odors. Similarly, they stay away from bad smells. So, things like cologne can make them stay away from us. For, staying away from filth is an attribute of pure spirits and angels. Today, there are many types of scents that do not contain alcohol and are, therefore, permissible. As is known, essences are extracted from various plants. Although some essences are produced through chemical methods using alcohol, it is possible to find essences that have been produced from plants. Therefore, there is no need to be in doubt when using such essences that are not dissolved with alcohol but with glucose. These do not invalidate prayers, and thus can be used instead of cologne or perfume with alcohol.

WHAT ARE THE THINGS THAT ARE ACCEPTED AS RITUALISTICALLY CLEAN?

- The earth and all kinds of mines and minerals, water, grass, trees, flowers, fruits, etc. on the earth, as well as the outer part of animals, unless polluted by something filthy, are accepted as pure. Only swine is exempted from this principle. For, the outer body, that is, the hair and skin of swine is impure as well as its meat. If a believer touches a pig with their hands or part of their garments, they must wash the part that has touched the animal as that part has been sullied. Followers of the Shafii School of Islamic jurisprudence also accept the outer part of the dog as filthy.

- The blood of lice, fleas and bedbugs are ritualistically clean.
- Fish and other animals that live and die in the water are clean. The blood of such animals is also clean and it does not contaminate garments.
- Even if the urine and feces of animals whose meat is edible in Islam is accepted as being light filth, their saliva is ritualistically clean.
- The skin, liver, heart, spleen, and blood of slaughtered animals are ritualistically clean. Blood that remains in their veins and meat and which does not flow out is also accepted as clean.
- Although the meat of animals that have been slaughtered in an un-Islamic way is unlawful, the parts of the body (other than swine) that do not have blood flowing through them are clean. Hence, the horns, hooves, bones, hair and tanned skin of such animals are accepted to be pure.
- Food, fat, meat or cheese which has gone off is not accepted as ritualistically impure. However, as they are harmful for the health, they are not consumed.
- The clothes that come into contact with the urine of domestic cats are considered clean although the urine of domestic cats contaminates vessels and the drinks inside them. Saliva of cats is not ritualistically impure.
- Urine drops as small as the point or eye of a needle do not make the body or clothes impure and do not invalidate the prayers. However, if this small amount of urine contaminates water, the water becomes ritualistically impure.

- Mud, whether solid or flowing, that is in the streets, is not impure, even if it contains dung. Clothes smeared with such mud are considered ritualistically clean.
- Water used for ablution or the complete ritualistic bath (*ghusl*) is pure. Such water can be used to eradicate filth. But it cannot be reused for ablutions or baths.
- Sleeping on the ground does not make clothes ritualistically impure.
- Wet garments that are put on something that is dirty but dry do not become impure provided that garments are not visibly smeared with the dirt.[6]

ARE ALL MARINE ANIMALS PURE?

Based on the verse, "*Lawful to you is the game of the sea and its food, as a provision for you,*" (Maeda 5:96) and the hadith, "Sea water is purifying and what dies in it is lawful,"[7] scholars are in agreement that among marine animals all fish are lawful. Some Islamic scholars like Imam Malik are of the opinion that all marine animals except those named after some terrestrial animals like sea hogs and sea dogs are lawful. According to the Hanafi School, only fish are lawful among the marine animals. All fish are lawful, whether they are taken out of water dead or alive, as the question of slaughtering them does not arise. The Messenger of God said: "What the sea throws up and is left by the tide you may eat, but what dies in the sea and floats you must not eat."[8] Accordingly, fish that die because of strong waves, hitting stones, being hunted, etc. are lawful, while those that die naturally without an external cause and begin to float on the surface of the water are considered unlawful.[9]

ARE PETS PERMISSIBLE IN ISLAM?

Every single creature deserves the recognition of being a creation of the Almighty, and all animals, as the creation of God, form "*communities like you*" (An'am 6:38). Islam has set a framework of how humanity should interact with its environment, with all other creatures and ecosystems that are *umma* (communities) in their own right like humankind. As attested by the Prophet Muhammad, "All creatures are like a family (*ayal*) of God, and He loves the most those who are the most merciful to His family.[10] As the sphere of human responsibility is extended to all living things, we should be merciful towards all living beings and help them for God's good pleasure.

As was reported by God's Messenger, a woman who was so cruel to her cat that she did not let it go out, eventually starving it to death was condemned to hell while a sinner was forgiven because of her mercy to a dog. She noticed a dog acting in a peculiar way as she climbed up a well after quenching her thirst. Remembering how she had felt only a few moments earlier, she climbed down again and filled her shoes with water and gave that water to the dog which was dying of thirst. This act, according to the Hadith, earned this woman enough reward to tip the scales in her favor and allowed her to enter Paradise.[11] As long as pets are not restricted in their liberty to go out or medically deprived of their right to mate and breed, pets are allowed in Islam, except that one must be careful about such pets which are *najis*. In addition, looking after a bird in a cage, although it is not a domestic bird or keeping a fish in an aquarium although it is not an aquarium fish means changing its inborn character and this is a form of cruelty. Such acts will be punished on the day when "the hornless sheep gets its claim from the horned sheep,"[12] as attested in the Hadith. It is cruel and therefore unlawful to inflict on them unpleasant situations or have them participate in any blood "sport" like hunting, dog or cock fighting, or to keep them in a cage so small that the animal cannot behave in a natural way.

Islam's concern for animals goes beyond the prevention of physical cruelty. It enjoins on the human to protect, employ with dignity, and promote the well-being of any animal in their care without any physical or psychological harm. The Prophet's companions asked, "O Messenger of God, do we have a reward for taking care of beasts?" He said, "There is a reward for acts of charity to every living crea ture."[13] Once another companion, Sawada narrated: "I went with my mother to the Prophet to ask for help. He gave us some goats and warned my mother: 'Tell your sons that they should cut their nails so that when they milk them, they will not hurt them and they will not bruise their breasts. Also, order your sons to prepare the food for their young well.'"[14]

As all animals are part of God's creation, including the ritual- istically impure pigs and dogs, it is a duty upon all of us not to ill- treat any of His creation. However, this does not mean that we should "love" and consider pets part of the family to the point that they are even preferred to people. Nowadays, more and more people think that they can only receive love whenever they want from pets, espe- cially dogs. People have come to rely on the dog more for compan- ionship and affection than anything else, and their display of exces- sive love for their dogs has reached the stage where there are bar- bers, private clubs, walking paths, cemeteries, lotions, shampoos, perfumes, and health insurance for dogs. The owners love their dogs that please them and want their dogs around them all the time. It is, however, unnatural to keep a dog as a companion to man, to have one that is small enough to carry around and sit on the lap like a child, rather than having children or being a member of the com- munity and helping the poor and needy. Islam is a religion that cares for people and does not encourage the idea that pets can replace human companionship in the process. We are instructed in numer- ous Hadiths not to keep dogs as pets[15] or to "love" them, something that is done by many people in various cultures today: "Almost six in 10 American households include a pet, compared with one in three that includes a child."[16] Unfortunately, dogs fill in for children in lots of the families, particularly in the West these days. The fol- lowing Hadith in this connection is most relevant, "When the Judgment Day is near, it will become more appealing to people to bring up the young of a dog than to bring up their own young." Many people, especially in Western societies have become very attached to their dogs which have become so much a part of the pattern of social life. In fact, it is impossible for this unnatural tradition not to hurt social relationships.

In Islam, there are certain restrictions in having a dog. Although dogs are considered to be impure and having a dog just for companionship is not recommended in Islam, a dog can be owned for some legitimate purposes and trained to do a variety of wonderful tasks as attested in the Qur'an: *"They ask you (O Muhammad) what is made lawful for them. Say: (all) good things are made lawful for you. And those beasts and birds of prey which you have trained as hounds are trained, you teach them that which God taught you; so eat of that which they catch for you and mention God's name upon it, and observe your duty to God. Surely, God is swift to take account"* (Maeda 5:4). So, Muslims can keep dogs for shepherding, security, or for game hunting. Such dogs have always been bred to perform specific tasks for their owners; there are hounds that are created to use their senses to find and chase prey, pointers and setters that flush out the prey, spaniels that flush and chase the prey, and retrievers that bring back the fallen prey. Dogs are also wonderful in search and rescue and in finding survivors in the rubble of earthquakes. The police and military frequently make use of dogs; for instance German shepherds, as they have a natural ability to defend and protect. Also, disabled people have a valid excuse to keep a dog that is clearly fulfilling a need; this is not the same as keeping a pet out of custom or love, and a guide dog becomes a blind person's eyes, therefore helping the disabled person achieve a level of independence.

The Prophet forbade close interaction with dogs, and he warned that they should not be kept without necessity. He also warned against allowing them to lick any part of the body, garments or food utensils. The saliva of a dog is impure, unlike that of a cat. So, if a dog licks a pot or a container, the food that the dog has touched and the food surrounding it must be thrown away. The remainder may be kept, as it is still pure. Also, the container should be washed seven times, as attested in a Hadith: "Purifying a container that a dog has licked is achieved by washing it seven times, the first time with pure soil, that is, water mixed with earth until it becomes muddy."[17] One may not substitute something else, like soap, in place of earth. Again, if the saliva of a dog touches the clothes or body, then that part of the body and/or the item of clothing that has been touched by the dog's mouth or snout has become ritually impure.

In brief, the traces of moisture on the body or clothes from either pigs or dogs, whether saliva, urine, or anything moist from them, must be purified in the way explained above as anything affected from their moisture prevents the performance of prayers.

WHAT IS THE RULING ON BRUSHES WITH PIG'S BRISTLE?

The Qur'an explicitly states that swine are filthy in and of themselves; *"For, that is surely unclean"* (An'am 6:145). Not only is their meat unclean, but also all parts of the pig are *"haram"* (unlawful). Although it is permissible to use, for instance, the skin of all other animals after tanning, including tanned skins of those animals whose meat is unlawful, this rule is not applicable to swine.[18] So, swine and all pork by-products and/or derivatives are unlawful.

In the past people were allowed to use pig bristle for making shoes as pig bristles enabled stitching to be carried out on shoes. Taking such a necessity into account, scholars such as Imam Abu Yusuf permitted the use of pig bristle only for making shoes and brushes. Just as in the case of making shoes, brushes made of pig bristle were allowed to paint rooms and houses. That is to say, painting done with a brush made of or shoes sewn with pig bristle is not considered filthy or impure. But the bristles must not have any contact with the human body.

Whether the use of pig bristle is still necessary today is disputable. Therefore, it is best for believers not to use such things as other alternatives are available. The pig is completely unclean (*najis*) and thus unlawful. It is not accepted as a trade commodity, for, it has no value. So, it cannot be sold or bought or used in anyway

WHAT IS THE RULING ABOUT WEARING MAKE-UP, USING HAIR DYE, HENNA, HAIR JELL, NAIL POLISH, LIPSTICK OR HAIR CREAM?

There are two aspects to this question. The first is the issue of whether or not women can wear makeup and adorn themselves. Women can adorn themselves within the limits prescribed by Islam. In Islam, women are allowed to adorn themselves only for their spouse, and in the past they were encouraged to use the cosmetics available at the time like henna and kohl. Women are also allowed to wear dresses made of silk and golden rings, bracelets, necklaces, and ear-rings.[19] But going outside among other people when wearing such ornaments is objectionable and forbidden.

The second is the issue of what the makeup has been made of. If it contains things that are not permissible in Islam, then it is unlawful to use the makeup. For example, if pig fat is used as an ingredient, or if the makeup creates a layer that is impermeable, like nail polish or some hair dyes, then it must not be used.

Nail polish and lipstick prevent water from reaching the nails and lips and some hair dyes hinder the hair from getting wet. Therefore, if you use hair dye you should be well informed about the type of dye you are using and should make sure that your hair gets wet when you make *ghusl* (complete ritual bath). If there are types of dye that do not prevent the hair from getting wet then there is no harm in using them. The same applies to hair creams. If these, too, do not form a covering on hair and cause it to remain dry, they can be used. Far from being unlawful, using henna is said to be a practice of the Prophet. This means that dyes like henna which do not form a new layer on the hair are undoubtedly permissible.

As for hair jells, if the jell applied to hair can be easily washed away with water and if the hair is thoroughly saturated, then using jells is not an obstacle to making the complete ritual bath. But it should be kept in mind that any kind of jells or dyes that prevent hair from becoming wet are obstacles for *ghusl*. People who use jells can decide for themselves. Does the hair remain upright and dry, rather than wet, because of the jell? Or is the jell washed away by water and the hair is clean and wet? The answer to this question will help us decide whether to use it or not.

What is the Ruling on Tattoos on the Body?

God's Messenger did not let people make drawings or figures on their skin and even warned that those who made tattoos or those who had somebody else do them would be the object of malediction. Yet, if someone previously had tattoos and later learns that they are not permissible in Islam, that person need not harm themselves by removing them unless the tattoo was of something obscene or a symbol opposed to the religion. Although there are many types of tattoos, generally they are made by injecting a color substance under the skin. Therefore, as it lies under the skin, a tattoo does not invalidate the ablution or ritual bath, for it does not cause the skin to remain dry.

But tattoos are not good for the health. An EU commission has stated that tattoos and piercing have become increasingly prevalent among European youth and that these have harmful effects on health. Medical specialists are also of the opinion that tattoos and piercing pose certain risks for health. Some of these risks are infection and the spread of hepatitis, AIDS, fungal infections, allergies, skin tumors, tuberculosis, tetanus, and skin cancer.

How can One Purify from Ritual Dirt?

Various means and methods can be used to purify things that are accepted as ritualistically unclean in Islam. The major means of purification are as follows:

A. Washing with Water

- Physical dirt can be purified with pure water, like that from rain, streams, wells and the sea, and by conditional water,[20] like flower water, rose water, or vegetable and fruit juice. When there is no water, even water which has been used for ablution can be re-used for cleansing.

- Visible filth is washed until its stain, that is its presence, odor and color, has been eradicated. The number of times it is washed is not important.

- If filth is something invisible like urine and does not leave a stain when dried out, the place that has been contaminated is washed in a vessel three times with different water each time and is wrung out. Yet, if it is not possible to wring out the contaminated object (like a mat, felt, or a carpet, etc.) then this object is washed in a vessel three times and dried each time. Such items should be hung until the water stops dripping. There is no need to wait until they are fully dried out before washing them again. If they are washed in a stream by letting water run over them and not in a vessel, then they should be washed until there is no trace of filth on them. There is no need for additional drying out.

B. Boiling in Water

- The way to purify meat that has been contaminated with filth is to remove its inner parts and boil it in clean water three times, changing the water each time. In this way, the filth inside the meat will be removed by the hot water and it will be purified.

- If tripe is put into boiling water without being washed first, it cannot be purified. But if it is put into water before the water boils, it can be purified by washing it in water several times and then can be boiled in clean water. The same rule applies if it is taken out of hot water that has not yet boiled, as it has not yet absorbed the water. That is, the tripe does not become unlawful. Washing will suffice to purify it.

- If poultry is slaughtered as prescribed by Islam and put into boiling water to pluck its feathers without first taking out the intestines, the filth inside it contaminates the meat, making it ritualistically impure. Therefore, after slaughtering such an animal, the flowing blood and unclean things inside it should be removed first and then the meat should be put into hot water. It is to be noted, however, if it is put into hot water and taken out without letting the filth contaminate the meat, the meat will not be unlawful.

C. PURIFYING WITH FIRE

- Things like earthenware water jugs, glasses and jars made of unclean clay can be put into fire to purify them.
- When filthy things, like dried dung and the like are burned and become ash, they are purified.

D. WIPING

- If things like knives, trays, glass, and varnished wood or plain marble are contaminated with wet or dry filth, they can be cleaned by wiping them with a wet piece of cloth or a sponge or something like earth. But it must be made certain that the filth has been completely removed.
- As for chiseled and decorated household items, such things cannot be purified by wiping. Only washing can purify them.

E. SCRAPING OR RUBBING

- The dried mark of semen on underwear or garments can be scraped off, and if the mark is still visible after scraping, this does not nullify acts of worship. However, a semen mark on the body cannot be cleaned by scraping or rubbing. It can only be purified by washing. Similarly, purity from wet sperm on the garment is only attained by washing.
- If solid fat is contaminated with something filthy, the contaminated part can be cut out and purified.

- If shoes or any light thin-soled boot that is worn indoors or inside overshoes, become filthy and if the filth is dry, then it can be scraped off. If the filth is wet, it must be washed off, or it can also be rubbed with a clean wet piece of cloth.
- If the filth is something invisible, like urine or wine, it should be washed and rubbed carefully with a soapy rag.

F. DRYING OUT STAINS

- If something like the earth, or a tree, or grass is soiled, it becomes clean when the dirt or filth dries out. Drying out can be done by sunlight, fire, or wind. Prayers can be performed on such a place, but such earth or sand cannot be used for *tayammum* (the substitution for *wudu,*' performed with sand or earth in case water is not available). For, although such places are pure, they cannot act as a purifier.
- Contaminated earth can be purified by pouring water or sprinkling clean earth over it until the mark or smell of the filth is gone.

G. FLOWING OR DIMINISHING OF WATER

- A small pool of contaminated water (for instance, the water in a paddling pool) can be purified by pouring clean water from an external source into the contaminated water until it overflows. This is in line with the judgment that streams do not become impure as long as they are flowing.
- Purifying a well can only be done by draining all the contaminated well-water.

H. CHANGING THE STATE OF A FILTHY SUBSTANCE

- If something filthy changes its state, it becomes purified. For example, if wine turns into vinegar with the addition of a chemical substance, it becomes pure. For in this way its essence has been changed.

- Soap made of impure olive oil is pure. However, cheese or yogurt made from impure milk is not pure, for its state has not been changed.

I. SLAUGHTERING AND TANNING

- As God's Messenger told us, the skin of all animals, no matter whether the animal has been slaughtered or died in a natural way, except for swine, becomes clean after it is tanned.[21] Thus, except for pig skin, the skin of those animals whose meat is unlawful can be used after it is tanned. Prayers can be performed on leather made of such skins.

> As reported by ibn 'Abbas, the Prophet's wife Sawda bint al-Zam'a said to the Prophet: "Our goat has died, O God's Messenger!" God's Messenger asked her: "Why didn't you take its skin?" Sawda said: "What shall we do the skin of a dead animal?" Upon this the Messenger explained: "God Almighty says, 'If you tan the skin of a dead animal, it is purified for you and you can use it.'" Sawda, peace be upon her, immediately got somebody to go and flay the skin of dead animal. She tanned it herself. Thus she used the purified skin as a water bag until it became worn out.

There are two ways of tanning:

1. Actual tanning: tanning done using compounds like alum, salt, and chemicals.

2. Ritualistic tanning: tanning by sprinkling earth over the skins or leaving them in the sun, air, or wind. Both ways are acceptable and prayers can be performed on skins tanned in either of these two ways. Skins that are known to have been tanned with something impure should be washed three times with water and are thus purified.

If it is doubtful as to whether or not the skin has been tanned with something impure, the hide is accepted as ritualistically pure. But it is better to wash it so as to get rid of any doubts or misgivings. Actually, if there are no clear signs that may lead to doubts, there is no need to investigate further. The skin is accepted as pure.

What are *Istinja* and *Istibra*?

Cleaning the private parts after relieving oneself is called *istinja,* while *istibra* means taking care that the flow of urine has fully ceased before making ablution. In particular, men must ensure that there are no drops of urine, for the emission of any urine after making the ablution, no matter how small the amount, invalidates the ablution. Some scholars have said that people who do not pay attention to this, even though they know the importance of the issue, are like those who deliberately perform prayers without ablution. Therefore, believers must be very sensitive about *istibra*. In a tradition, the Prophet says, "Be careful of urine for most of the torment in the grave is from that,"[22] and thus warns believers to take great care about cleansing after urination.

Although *istinja* (cleaning the private parts) can be done with toilet paper when there is no water, doing *istinja* with water and using toilet paper to dry the private parts is certainly the best way.

In order to be sure on this matter men can adopt habits that are recommended in Islamic books of jurisprudence such as coughing, taking a brisk walk, gently pressing one's penis, or placing a tissue in one's underwear, etc.[23]

The Good Manners of *Istinja* and *Istibra*

First of all, the proper behavior necessary when relieving oneself must be learnt. Manners concerning relieving oneself are as follows:

- Before entering the toilet anything on which God's name is written, such as rings, must be taken off. Pieces of paper on which Qur'anic verses are written must also be taken out of the pockets and put somewhere clean. If there is nowhere to put them outside the toilet, then these should be wrapped inside a plastic bag and put into a pocket.

- Before entering the toilet, it is recommended to say *"Bismillah"* and recite this prayer: *"Allahumma inni a'udhu bika min al-khubthi wal-khaba'ith"* (My Lord! I take refuge in You from all filth and filthy things.)

- Step into the toilet with the left foot first and leave by putting the right foot first.

- Turn neither your front nor your back towards the direction of *qibla*. This is abominable.

- Unless necessary, do not speak in the toilet. Neither mention spiritual or sacred things, nor return a greeting.

- It is not recommended to urinate in a standing position unless you have a valid excuse. Urinating in a sitting position is the best way. For in this way the bladder empties more easily. This will reduce dripping and leakage of urine.

- Do not look at one's private parts or the excrement.

- After leaving the toilet, it is good manners to say: *"Alhamdu lillahilladhi adhhaba 'anil-adha wa 'afani"* (Thanks to God, Who makes me rid myself of the things that bother me and Who makes me sound and healthy.)

ABOMINABLE (*MAKRUH*) THINGS ABOUT *ISTINJA*

- It is abominable (*makruh*) to urinate towards the wind or into stagnant or flowing water. It is also forbidden to urinate or relieve oneself under fruit trees or in the shade of other trees, in crop fields, on the nest of ants and insects, or on roads. As this would bother people and therefore make them curse or swear, relieving oneself on thoroughfares or under the shade of trees was especially prohibited by the Prophet, peace and blessings be upon him.

It is also not proper to leave the toilet without having cleaned it. After defecating, people should clean the toilet thoroughly. Neglecting this is annoying for other people.

Only the left hand should be used while cleaning the private parts. In a tradition the Prophet, peace and blessings be upon him, says: "none of you should touch his genitals with his right hand while urinating. He should not wipe (his private parts) with his right hand after reliving himself, either." Because of this hadith, scholars believe that cleaning private parts with right hand is abominable (*makruh*).

- While cleaning after defecation, water should not be splashed around.
- If there a risk that the private parts may be seen, *istinja* can be neglected.
- It is not permissible to urinate in places where ritualistic baths (*ghusl*) are taken. It is said that "most of the apprehension and misgivings result from this." However, some scholars say that urination is permissible in places where water does not form a pool and where it easily flows away. In any case, believers should be cautious.

THE GREATEST BLESSING IN THE WORLD

It has been narrated that an Ottoman Sultan visited Laleli Baba, a saint whose every word was said to be full of wisdom. People had no doubts about the man's sainthood. After asking many questions and receiving answers, the Sultan asked a final question: "What is the greatest blessing in the world?" "Relieving oneself after eating and drinking is the greatest blessing," the man said.

Not very pleased with this answer, the Sultan left and returned to his palace. After eating and drinking many things, the Sultan could not relieve himself. He could not sleep until morning. At dawn he made ablution and performed the dawn prayer. After the prayer he ran directly to the house of Laleli Baba. He said he had not been able to sleep the whole night and begged him to pray on his behalf to be saved from this difficulty.

Laleli Baba said, "Although God grants us many blessings, we do not recognize their value because of our habits. Now you know how great a blessing it is to be able to relieve oneself after eating and drinking, do you not?" He went on and said, "If you dedicate this mosque of yours to me and give me your sultanate, I will pray so that you may be saved from this distress." The Sultan immediately agreed to dedicate the mosque and called it "Laleli Mosque," but refused to give up his sultanate. But soon he relented and agreed to hand over the entire empire to Laleli Baba. Laleli Baba said, "What kind of sultanate is this? A sultanate that is given in exchange for relieving oneself...!"

Laleli Baba prayed for the Sultan and he was saved from his condition. The mosque has been known as Laleli Mosque ever since.

Thinking about this story should help us realize the invaluable things that have been granted to us by God and to understand how valuable it is for us to be able to relieve ourselves.

WHAT ARE THE TYPES OF WATER THAT CAN BE USED FOR CLEANSING?

There are in general two types of water: Absolute, pure water and conditional water.

1. Absolute, pure water

Kinds of water such as that from rain, snow, wells, seas, lakes, rivers, springs, and reservoirs are known as absolute water. When we say "water," these types of pure water first come to mind. Only these types of water can be used for ablution and ritual baths.

2. Conditional water

This is a type of water that has lost its essential form after becoming combined with some other substance and gaining a new name, such as rose water, flower water, fruit juice, meat broth, etc.

If absolute, pure water is mixed with conditional water and attains a few of the characteristics from the conditional water, such as color, odor, or taste, it is accepted as conditional. Conditional water cannot be used to perform ablution and take ritual baths. That is to say, it cannot be used to eliminate impurity. For, God Almighty has ordained that only pure water should be used for ritual cleansing.

Absolute, pure water remains pure even if it is mixed with such ritually pure things as sand and soil, on the condition that it does not loses it fineness or fluidity.

CHAPTER 3

Physical Cleanliness

A. Cleanliness of the Body and Garments

The word *tahara* has many connotations, all of which are positive; the word means purity and purification from filth, and as far as bodily cleanliness or personal hygiene is concerned, *tahara* includes the cleansing of the skin, hands, mouth, nose, ears, eyes, etc. and care of the hair, beard, nails, armpits, private parts, face, teeth, and feet. The Prophet Muhammad paid great attention to the care of the nails, hair, beard, and mustache and the cleanliness of the armpits and private parts.[1]

People expect others to be tidy and clean, no matter whether they themselves are clean or not. Cleanliness or the state of being clean is a prerequisite for being respected and relied upon. God's Messenger warns those who do not pay attention to tidiness and cleanliness:[2] "One of you asks me about the Heavens, but he has long nails under which filth and food remnants have gathered," and points to the social aspect of cleanliness when he says: "Do not come near me with yellow teeth and foul breath."[3]

The General Cleansing of Body

The general cleansing of the body entails washing the body with warm water and soap in order to purify the skin from filth and excretions. Believers should take baths everyday or every other day, or at least once a week. *Ghusl* (a complete ritualistic bath), which is obligatory in Islam, is an important means of bodily cleansing and believers are advised by God's Messenger to wash their body completely at least once a week and purify themselves from every kind dirt and filth.

It is known that contact with water balances the static energy in the body and that baths with warm water reduce and heal aches and some rheumatic diseases. Warm water also reduces stress, gives relief and energy, enhances blood circulation and is beneficial for healthy skin. Some of these benefits can also be attained with cold showers or baths. It is recommended for health that those who cannot take cold showers should at least wash their hands, arms, face, feet, and legs with cold water after a hot shower. Bathing with very hot water or too much scrubbing with a coarse bath glove is not advisable for the health of the skin. Common pools and stagnant water should also be avoided, except for those used for medical purposes as there may be some risk to the health.

As for personal hygiene, we should wash our hands when we get up in the morning, before and after meals, before preparing food and cooking, after contact with animals, after changing diapers, before and after looking after patients, etc. Washing the face reduces headaches, regulates the blood circulation in the head and thus helps us lead a healthy, energetic life. Also, washing the neck as well as the face stimulates the veins that feed the brain and is therefore very important.

Cleanliness of feet is also very important for health. The feet must be washed every day and must be dried thoroughly each time. Otherwise, dampness will cause fungus to grow. Toenails must be cut regularly. Shoes must not be too small and socks or stockings must be made of a quality material that absorbs sweat. The cleanliness of shoes is also very important. Shoes absorb the smell and sweat of feet and when they are worn, the feet immediately get dirty. Therefore, not only feet, but also shoes and socks must be kept clean.

The cleanliness of nails is an important part of the cleanliness of hands and feet. The nails on the hand should be cut short and round, while toenails should be cut straight so that they do not lead to ingrown toenails.

It must not be forgotten that nails can be a host to germs. To underline this fact the Prophet, peace and blessings be upon him, said: "O Ali, cut your long nails, for harmful things live under long nails."[4] Today we know that some of these harmful organisms are germs. The fact that we use our hands to do many things means that the cleanliness of nails is even more important. Usually, it is sufficient to cut one's nails once a week.

Moreover, God's Messenger said: "There are ten acts according to *fitrat* (natural disposition): clipping the moustache, letting the beard grow, using the *miswak*, sniffing water into the nose, rinsing the mouth, cutting the nails, washing between the fingers, shaving or plucking the hair under the armpits, shaving pubic hairs and cleaning one's private parts with water."[5] In this hadith, God's Messenger lists the cutting of nails as an act of natural cleanliness.

Another matter mentioned in the above hadith, cleaning inside the nose, also has positive benefits, as it makes inhalation easier and helps the lungs get fresh air. The system that warms air is stimulated and it works more efficiently. Lakit ibn Sabira asked the Prophet to teach him how to perform ablution. The Prophet said, "Perform ablution thoroughly, rub the parts between your fingers, sniff water into your nose if you are not fasting."[6] This is important advice concerning the cleansing of the nose. The Prophet said: "When any one of you wakes up from sleep and performs ablution, he must clean his nose three times."[7] However, it is important not to do it loudly or to annoy people while doing it. Also, cleaning the nostrils with fingers and removing nose hair in the presence of others is rude and is a bad habit. It is not correct to blow one's nose on the roads, pavements, or anywhere that can be seen by other people. Islam is not only a religion of cleanliness, but also one of good manners.

CLEANLINESS OF THE MOUTH AND TEETH

We must brush our teeth with a toothbrush or a *miswak* to get rid of food remnants from between our teeth and the bacteria on our gums. Brushing our teeth is the easiest and cheapest way of ensuring a healthy mouth and healthy teeth. Brushing must be done from the gums towards teeth thoroughly and the brush must be changed every three months for hygiene. Rinsing the mouth with water or drinking some water after eating or drinking something that contains glucose or carbohydrate will protect the teeth against rotting. We should go to a dentist and have our teeth checked regularly.

The sensitivity of God's Messenger about the health of the mouth and teeth is very noteworthy. As he advised the use of *miswak* (a twig of the tree *araq*, which is naturally sweet-smelling) during ablution, it can be concluded from the number of obligatory and non-obligatory prayers that he advised believers to use the *miswak* several times a day. He used to perform supererogatory *duha* (broad daylight) prayer and clean his teeth with *miswak* while performing ablution and just before beginning to perform the other prayers. He said: "Were it not that I might over-burden the believers, I would have ordered them to use *miswak* at every prayer."[8] "Use *miswak*, for it is purification for the mouth."[9] He would also use *miswak* before going to sleep and upon waking, as well as before performing ablution.[10]

We should be diligent in this matter and brush our teeth several times a day. In another hadith God's Messenger says:

> Cleanse your teeth with *miswak*. For, it is purification for the teeth and a means of seeking God's pleasure. Gabriel recommended that I use the *miswak* every time he came. So much so that I began to fear that it would become obligatory for my *umma*. If I had not thought it hard for my followers or the people, I would have ordered them to clean their teeth with *miswak* for every prayer. I use *miswak* so relentlessly that it seems as if my teeth (or my gum) will be scraped off.[11]

This hadith, reported by forty different people, clearly shows that *miswak* is a Sunna of God's Messenger and has many benefits. So this Prophetic practice should be followed by believers. Using *miswak* is important as a preventive measure and will continue to be so in the future. We know of no other saying which stresses the importance of cleansing the teeth as much as this hadith does. In another hadith he says, "Surely your mouths are ways for the Qur'an. Clean them with *miswak*"[12] He also says, "God is Graceful and He loves Grace."[13] *Latif*, which means "beautiful" is one of God's attributes.

He does not like what is ugly. So believers must keep their mouth clean so as to be loved by God. Using *miswak* is among the sunna of ablution in the Hanafi School and among that of the prayers for the Shafii School. In any case, believers should brush their teeth with *miswak* or toothbrush whenever they perform ablution for the prayers.

Although the word *miswak* is used in the Prophet's sayings, it is clear that the main point that is stressed is the cleansing of the teeth. This can be done in any way, rubbing with fingers, using a tooth brush, or dental floss. On the other hand, the importance of *miswak* lies in the fact that it contains fluorine, which is useful for teeth health. Studies about *miswak* have shown that some enzymes excreted by the essence of *miswak* are protective against germs, that it protects teeth enamel, feeds the gums, and that it is also useful for the stomach because of its sweet smell. Certainly, if cleansing the mouth is done with God's good pleasure in mind, the importance of religious rules for our daily life will be better understood.

Cleanliness of the mouth is not only something to do with physical cleanliness. A believer must pay attention not only to the physical cleaning of their mouth, tongue, and teeth, but also to their spiritual purity. It is notable that *dhikr* (remembrance of God) and *tasbih* (praising God), as well as refraining from telling lies, uttering obscene words, bad language, backbiting, and slandering, as well as refraining from eating *haram*, or unlawful food is much more important than the physical cleanliness of the mouth.

THE IMPORTANCE OF ABLUTION FOR PHYSICAL CLEANLINESS

In addition to the types of cleanliness mentioned above, Muslims must have ablution to perform the prayers. Ablution is beneficial as a preventive measure, for many diseases spread through the mouth and nose. Also, ablution includes most elements of hydrotherapy,[14] which has recently become very popular.

God has ordained Muslims to perform ablution and *ghusl* (major canonical ablution) when in ritually impure states.[15] This is another reason for being thankful to God, for in everything ordained by God, there are many benefits.

GOLD-PLATED TEETH

This issue can be discussed from different perspectives. If a man or a woman wants to plate their teeth, even though they have healthy teeth, this is certainly not permissible in Islam.

According to Imam Muhammad and Imam Abu Yusuf, if a tooth cavity is filled and if there is a medical necessity for the tooth to be plated, and if in this case silver or other metals have the risk of producing bacteria inside the mouth, then it is permissible to plate the teeth with gold under the guidance of a religious dentist. But Abu Hanifa is of a different opinion in this matter. According to him, gold is never permissible. On the other hand, the two afore-mentioned Imams tell of Arfaja among the Companions, who had a nose made of gold as he lost his nose during battle. Because of the possibility of infection, a new nose was made of gold for him and the Prophet consented to this. Showing this incidence as a proof for their argument, the two imams claim that men can have gold-plated teeth in case of necessity.[16] In short, if dentists approve of the necessity, teeth can be gold-plated.

Teeth have a very important role in human health. They are of crucial importance. Therefore, it is not wise to have every aching tooth extracted. Availing ourselves of technology is one of our duties. Actually, caring for our teeth so as to maintain their health and preventing a loss of teeth is the best thing we can do. It should also be noted that though gold plating can be done as explained above, new technology allows teeth to be covered in other ways.

Some people have extremist views about this issue. They understand the principle of washing the inner part of the mouth according to the Hanafi School as "washing inside of the teeth" and take this as a proof for their argument. On the contrary, washing only the inside of the mouth is obligatory while performing *ghusl* according to the Hanafi School. This means that water need only contact the outer part of the teeth. In fact, Islam has such broad views that it even allows those with broken arms or legs to lightly wipe the plaster on the broken limb, as it cannot be washed.

CLEANLINESS OF THE HAIR, BEARD, AND MUSTACHE

Cleanliness of the hair is important for health, as some germs and parasites can stick to dirty hair and skin more easily. Hair should be washed every day or every other day; if this is not possible at least twice a week to prevent it from becoming greasy and unhealthy. We should avoid irritating the scalp and the roots of the hair, for this may increase the production of oils. The hair, beards, and mustaches should be combed, regularly trimmed, and kept clean. Dyes should be avoided, for the chemicals in them may harm hair.

God's Messenger used to clean and comb his hair very carefully. He did not like uncombed or dirty hair. One day, a dirty man with unkempt and uncombed hair came into his presence. Seeing this man, he said: "Didn't this man have enough water to wash his hair or enough oil to tidy it?" then added "He who has hair should honor it."[17] Thus, the Prophet emphasized the importance of the tidiness and cleanliness of hair.

As for care of a mustache, the Prophet, peace and blessings be upon him, advised his companions to trim the part of mustache that covers the upper lip. The mustache should be trimmed so it does not get food in it.

It seems appropriate not to make broad generalizations concerning the issue of cutting hair so as not to cause misunderstandings. It would be more appropriate to mention related reports and comment on them briefly. Some reported sayings of the Prophet are as follows:

Ibn 'Umar narrated, "The Prophet, peace and blessings be upon him, saw a boy with part of his head shaved and part left unshaven. He forbade them to do that, saying: "Shave it all or leave it all."[18] Again as reported by ibn 'Umar, God's Messenger prohibited believers to shave part of the head and leave the rest unshaved.[19]

The Prophet, peace and blessings be upon him, used to look after children's hair. Narrated by Abdullah, son of Ja'far, "Three days after the death of Ja'far, the Prophet, peace and blessings be upon him, came to visit them, and said: 'Do not weep over my brother after this day,' and he said: 'Call to me the children of my brother.' We were brought to him as if we were chicken. He said: 'Call me a barber.' He then ordered that our heads be shaved."[20]

God's Messenger informed his followers of not to wear artificial hair. Narrated by Asma, daughter of Abu Bakr, "A woman came to God's Messenger and said, 'I married my daughter to someone, but she became sick and all her hair fell out, and (because of that) her husband does not like her. Can she use false hair?' On that the Prophet cursed people who supply false hair and those who ask for it.

Concerning general appearance, Fethullah Gülen, a contemporary Islamic scholar, provides us with a clear understanding of the matter:

> As is reported in many books about the life of the Prophet, most companions of God's Messenger had long, braided hair. Some of them would gather it in a knot. In Bukhari's Al-Sahih, the following incidence is narrated: 'Seeing a man who had knotted his hair during Hajj, the Prophet advised him to untie his hair so that his hair, also, got the benefit from "sajda". God's Messenger ordered neither Abu Bakr, nor 'Umar, nor 'Uthman, all of whom had long hair, to cut their hair.
>
> After the conquest of Mecca, the hearts of many people were softened and warmed towards Islam with rewards and most of them embraced Islam. They had garments in the style of non-believers and the turban of unbelievers on their heads. The Prophet did not want them to remove even these. Indeed, this would be formalism and he was far beyond formalism. He did not give any orders that may be taken as formalism.
>
> Actually, outer appearance is not something essential in Islam, but something of secondary importance. So, we should not be too concerned with outer appearance and formalism. The Prophet may have warned those who had cut some parts of their hair and left other parts, just as some young people do today, thus distorting the natural appearance, so that they would not imi-

tate the nonbelievers. As is mentioned in the sections of hadith books concerning garments and physical appearance, mainly in Tirmidhi, the Prophet used to comb his hair according to the customs of the time in Mecca so as not to resemble the unbelievers. After he emigrated to Medina and saw that Christians and Jews there combed their hair over their forehead (like those in historical pictures and films about Romans), he changed the way he combed his hair again and parted it in the middle and combed it to the right and to the left. Probably, some people used to cut the sides and grow hair only the top and this was an imitation of Christians and Jews. Therefore, the Prophet behaved in accordance with the hadith, "He who imitates any people is one of them."[21]

The human body is formed in a perfect manner. It is formed with such subtle rules of geometry and mathematics that it is impossible not to appreciate it. Most probably, it is not right to change something that has been created in such a perfect manner. In a hadith, the Prophet, peace and blessings be upon him, says: "God wants to see the signs of His blessing on His servants."[22] Therefore, it would not be incorrect to say that hair should be cut in a way that is suitable to its natural form.

But today, some needless interventions may have negative effects, even on devoted believers. Therefore, nobody must take the place of the Prophet and say, "Cut your hair, tidy your clothes" or any other negative comments on appearance. This is not the way it should be said. If you say such things, they will go away and will never return to your world of thought.[23]

CLEANLINESS AND A GOOD APPEARANCE

A group of the Prophet's Companions came together and visited him. They stopped at the door of the Messenger's house, which was next to the mosque, and asked for permission to enter the house.

The Prophet was having a rest at home. When he was told that he had visitors, he immediately got dressed and walked towards the door to meet his guests. Next to the door was a large jar full of water. Before opening the door, he leaned towards the jar and seeing his reflection on the water, tidied his hair and turban.

Aisha, the Prophet's wife, was surprised to see that the Prophet was tidying his hair and clothes before opening the door for a group of Muslims. She could not help asking, "O God's Messenger! Do you, too, preen yourself?" The Prophet, who lived a perfect Islamic life and established a perfect example for us, said: "Yes, O Aisha! A Muslim must tidy himself before going to the presence of his brothers. God is beautiful and loves those whose inside and outside is beautiful. God wants Muslims to appear beautiful to their brothers."

This means that being untidy or shabby is not a characteristic of Muslims. Contrary to some people's belief, shabby clothes and untidiness is not an indication of modesty or virtue. Nowadays, some people spread the false idea that Muslims should be indifferent or unheeding towards worldly affairs and Muslims who wear shabby clothes enforce this false idea. It will make people think that such shabbiness is recommended or ordained by the religion. So, being shabby will cause negative attitudes not only towards ourselves, but also our religion. Wearing clean and tidy clothes is the *sunna* of the Prophet. Therefore, we must tidy and clean our bodies and clothes before we meet our friends and brothers in religion.

CLEANLINESS OF OUR PRIVATE PARTS

The private parts of our bodies should always be kept clean. The Prophet said: "When anyone among you wakes up from sleep, he must wash his hands three times, for he does not know what his hands were during the night"[24] This saying of the Prophet is directly related to the parts of body where there is excretion and sweat, providing the most suitable conditions for bacteria.

We can understand that while sleeping people can touch their private parts and after they awake they can spread germs if they do not wash their hands.

The Prophet also counted among the acts of *fitrat* the trimming or shaving of armpit and pubic hair and using water to wash private parts after relieving oneself.[25] The cleansing of private parts after a bowel movement is carried out with just toilet paper in most

Western countries. As water is not used, if the pubic hair is not cut, it becomes very difficult to clean the private parts thoroughly. Some claim that it is more hygienic to use toilet paper without using water for cleaning the private parts. In Western style toilets there is no connection to any water source other than the tank. Later, a water connection with a little hose for cleansing the private parts next to the toilet started to be added. In this way, toilet paper can be used before and after washing with water, especially for drying the private parts after washing with water for thorough cleansing. *Istinja* (cleaning the private parts) should be done with left hand and abundant water should be used. The People of Quba in Madina were using water to do *istinja* and the following verse in the Qur'an was revealed about them: *"...in it are men who love that they should be purified; and God loves those who purify themselves"* (Tawba 9:108). And the Prophet asked: "O community of *Ansar*! God praises you over your cleanliness. What is your cleanliness that it deserves such praise?" They said, "We perform ablution before the prayers, have a bath when we are ritually impure and wash our private parts with water." Then the Prophet said: "The praise is for this. Therefore continue to do so."[26]

The Prophet's wife, Aisha reported that God's Messenger never left the toilet without first performing *istinja* with water. Also, ibn 'Umar said: "We did the same and saw that this was a means for healthiness and cleanliness."[27]

Trimming hair in the pubic area or under the armpits in a state of ritual impurity as a result of sexual intercourse is abominable (*makruh*). For such cleansing should be done before the *ghusl* (bath of purification) becomes obligatory, that is, before sexual relations.

CLEANLINESS DURING MENSES AND PREGNANCY

As hygiene of the genitals is important for everyone and particularly for young girls, they should be taught to cleanse the genitals with water, starting first from the front of the genitals to the rear, so as to avoid urethra infections.

For such cleansing, women should be advised to use cleansers with a neutral pH instead of soap. During menstruation damp pads should be changed frequently so as to avoid diseases. Wearing underwear and trousers made of polyester or other synthetic material also increases the risk of infection. It is beneficial to have a shower every day during such a time. Young girls should be taught to use absorbent pads when they reach the age of puberty. Hygienic pads placed inside the underwear are the best protectors. In the first days of menstruation, when there is more blood, pads should be changed more frequently. Girls should be taught that neglecting the changing of pads may lead to discomfort or even illness. Even when there is little blood, a pad should not be used for more than eight hours.

As the sebaceous and sweat glands are more active during pregnancy, pregnant women should have showers frequently. Having showers with warm water is safer than having a bath in the bath-tub to avoid infections during pregnancy. Similarly, public baths can be risky for pregnant women.[28]

CLEANLINESS OF GARMENTS

The selection and upkeep of clothes is very important for personal hygiene; fabrics of natural fibers and cotton should be chosen over synthetic ones to help prevent infections.

During the Middle Ages, Europeans used to wear woolen clothes, which keep one warm but are difficult to clean, and they rarely had baths. Thus, to mask foul smells, people used perfumes made of herbs and flowers. In the eighteenth-century the cotton trade began in Europe and Europeans began to use cheap, light and easily washable underwear for the first time. Bathing and personal hygiene became prevalent in the West, especially with interior plumbing in the twentieth century. The cleansing of body and clothes destroyed lice and fleas and eliminated diseases such as the plague and typhus.

Although the importance of wearing clean clothes first began to be understood in the nineteenth century in the West, Muslims who led a true Islamic life have been paying great care to the cleanliness of their clothes since the 7ᵗʰ century.[29] For Muslims, cleanliness of their clothes is one the prerequisites for performing prayers. That is to say, Muslims have to check whether their garments are clean or not five times a day. For instance, the prayers cannot be performed with clothes that are contaminated with urine or feces. The Prophet's following saying clearly shows the importance he attached to the cleanliness of clothes: "Wear white clothes, for white clothes are more beautiful and more suitable for cleanliness. Shroud your dead with such cloth, as well."[30] Stains and dirt are more easily visible on light-colored clothes, so greater care is needed to keep them clean. Accordingly, we should pay attention to the cleanliness of not only our body, but also of our clothes, and thus follow the example of our beloved Prophet.

CAN ONE PRAY IN READY-MADE CLOTHES BEFORE WASHING THEM?

In Islam, when there is no direct prohibition about something, it is accepted to be essentially permissible. Hence, ready-made clothes and tailor-made clothes are ritualistically clean unless there is proof that they are not. But if the clothes or the fabric of the clothes is dirty, it must be cleaned according to Islamic rules.

ARE THE CLOTHES RITUALLY CLEAN AFTER DRY-CLEANING?

Guidelines concerning cleanliness are clearly explained in books of Islamic jurisprudence. According to these guidelines, if there is dirt on clothes, they should be washed until the dirt disappears. If the dirt has penetrated into the fabric and if it does not disappear, the cloth should be washed three times and wrung out. Also clothes soiled with dirt that is not visible should be washed three times and wrung out.

When a garment that is not ritually dirty (*najis*) is washed with one that is ritually dirty, the one which is not dirty (*najis*) becomes impure and the same rules of cleansing apply to it.[31] If dry cleaners pay attention to these rules, the clothes they clean are ritualistically pure.

What is the Ruling on Detergents Used to Clean Clothes?

There are several aspects involved in this issue:

1. The ingredients of detergents can be identified by chemists. If the alcohol used in detergents is pure, it is not permissible to use it. But if it becomes part of a compound, with other chemicals and changes in essence, the detergent can be used.

2. Science is developing with an astounding speed. Therefore, its truths are continuously changing. So it is difficult to make judgments about issues in which there are no absolute truths. For instance, in the past aluminum pots and pans were said to be harmless and this was considered a scientific fact, but recently they have been discovered to cause cancer. Detergents, too, have similar risks for health. Scientists assert that some kinds of dishwashing detergents can cause skin diseases. Even if there is nothing impermissible by religion in the ingredients of the detergent, we must be aware that they may cause various diseases. Moreover, our knowledge is limited; this is all we know today. But what will be found out about this issue is something nobody can know.

3. Another aspect of this issue is one pertaining to Islamic jurisprudence. According to Islamic sources, while light dirt (*najasa al-khafifa*) is cleansed in simple ways, anything smeared with heavy dirt (*najasa al-ghaliza*) must be washed, rinsed, and wrung at least three times,[32] otherwise it is not ritualistically pure. What is more, deducing from the hadith that a vessel licked by a dog must be washed seven times, one of which should be done with clean earth, the Shafii School of Islamic jurisprudence has commented that such things must be washed seven times.[33] In relation to this matter, it

is better to follow this opinion of the Shafii School and act accordingly.

In short, technology facilitates our life on the one hand, but leads to many controversies on the other. Therefore, we should not decide in haste on such matters and say "this is permissible and that is not." We should be cautious in such matters.

WHAT IS THE RULING ON PRAYING IN CLOTHES SMEARED WITH FILTH?

First of all, believers should arrange their life in accordance with the acts of worship. People who have to work in places where there is a high risk of getting contaminated with heavy dirt (*najasa al-ghaliza*) like pig fat should keep an extra set of clothing for daily prayers. Even covering the body between the navel and the knees is better for men than wearing dirty clothes when performing daily prayers. Prayers cannot be performed with dirty clothes unless there is no other possibility. One of the prerequisites of the prayers is to purify oneself from dirt. Another possibility for those working in such places is to wear overalls at work and take them off when performing prayers.

B. CLEANLINESS OF FOOD AND DRINKS

GENERAL INFORMATION ABOUT CLEANLINESS OF FOOD AND DRINKS

Most germs and parasites pass into the human body via food and drink. Therefore, we must be very careful about food hygiene, particularly those of us who work in the food sector. The main source of bacteria that causes food poisoning is the human body. The throat, nose, hands, skin, intestines, and feces are all covered with bacteria.

Human beings attain most of their food from animals. Such nutrients may sometimes contain bacteria. Domestic animals like dogs, cats, etc. can also spread bacteria. Domestic animals carry bacteria wherever they wander. Flies, insects, and mice also carry infectious germs. Garbage left in kitchens is a suitable environment for germs to breed. Bacteria can spread from garbage that is not disposed of in time to our food via insects, flies, and mice. To prevent the spread of bacteria we should:

– Wash our hands.

– Clean our nose.

– Cut our nails.

– Wash our hands thoroughly after going to the toilet.

– Cover food and drink vessels.

Food must be protected against saliva and mucus, which can be transmitted via sneezing and coughing. There are 100 million bacteria in a gram of saliva and 10 million in mucus. 30% to 50% of all people carry a kind of bacteria (staphylococcus aurous) in their nose, which causes food poisoning. This figure rises to 65% to 80% among those who work in hospitals. Bacteria in the mouth, nose, and respiratory system spread in the air via respiration. This diffusion is less while speaking. When coughing, sneezing, or speaking loudly the number of bacteria that spread to the air increases.

With a strong cough, about 5,000 particles are released from the body. In a sneeze, this number increases to one million. These particles can stay in a hanging position for several hours. When someone carrying food sneezes or coughs, the bacteria in their mouth can spread to the food.

Someone coughing at home can pass their germs to open vessels. Moreover, food and drink vessels must be kept covered to prevent bacteria spreading from domestic animals, flies, insects, and rodents. Apartment blocks and flats are not the only places where people live. Most people lived in single story houses or tents for hundreds of years; many still live in such environments. Therefore, they have very close contact with domestic animals, flies, and rodents. Covering food vessels will prevent these animals from spreading diseases. Insects that live in central heating equipment in apartments and flats live on food remnants in the kitchen and also spread disease. To prevent this, garbage must be disposed of as soon as possible and food must be protected against domestic animals.

The Prophet's commands and advice concerning washing the hands after going to the toilet, cleansing the nose, and cutting nails have great importance in preventative medicine. Here, some other Prophetic sayings concerning the protection of vessels against bacteria must be remembered, as well. "Cover the vessels and tie the water skin, for there is a night in a year when pestilence descends, and it does not pass an uncovered vessel or an untied water skin but some of that pestilence descends into it."[34] This hadith tells us about covering vessels not only against certain germs, but also states that all kinds of germs can spread in the air and contaminate vessels. Coughing while carrying an open vessel of food may also cause infection.[35]

Many epidemic diseases are introduced to human beings via the things they eat or drink. Therefore, we must be very careful about the protection of food and drinks from different germs and bacteria and be very cautious in the matter of hygiene.

WHAT IS THE RULING ABOUT ANIMALS THAT ARE NOT SLAUGHTERED IN THE NAME OF GOD?

Muslims cannot eat meat from animals that are slaughtered in the name of others than God. Mentioning God's name while slaughtering an animal means that the permission is renewed and God's infinite power and will is remembered, as it is only He Who gives and takes the life of all creatures and He Who gives human beings the permission to slaughter animals. Some other wisdom behind this prohibition is that it is aimed to eradicate paganism and enforce faith in God's Oneness. God Almighty declares clearly in the Qur'an that the meat of animals slaughtered in the name of others than God is unlawful (*haram*):

> He has only forbidden you what dies of itself, and blood, and
> flesh of swine, and that over which any other name than that of
> God has been invoked (Baqara, 2:173).

WHAT IS THE WISDOM BEHIND ACCEPTING PORK AS UNLAWFUL?

Just as performing daily prayers and observing the fast are acts of worship, so too are refraining from consuming pork and all pork by-products and/or derivatives and drinking alcoholic drinks. According to the prominent Islamic scholar, Bediüzzaman Said Nursi, obligations are the established acts of worship (*muthba ibada*), while prohibitions are the protective acts of worship (*manfi ibada*). The basis of both established and protective acts of worship is "God's decree," the result is "God's good pleasure," and "the yield pertains to the Hereafter." That is, when carrying out God's commands, it is essential to expect rewards in the Hereafter. Therefore, as servants of God we must act according to the admonitions and prohibitions of God and avoid prohibited things in the same way that we avoid Satan.

God is not only the Sovereign and the Absolute, eternal Authority over everything but He is also *Al-Hakim* (the All-Wise), in Whose every act and decree there are many instances of wisdom, as none of His decrees is futile. Numerous remarks can be made about the prohibition of pork. On this issue, it seems appropriate to underline one or two points that can be easily found in encyclopedias.

The bacterium called trichina takes two different forms in the flesh of swine, namely as a cist and as larva. The cist is the immature form of trichina and the larva is the mature form. This bacterium, which camouflages itself inside a capsule, lives inside the muscles of swine. Trichina passes to the body of those who eat pork and causes many diseases. According to doctors, this bacterium goes the stomach in the form of a cist and it gets dissolved in acid. It passes to the intestines and multiplies in number through insemination, producing up to somewhere between 2,250 to 2,500 germs. These trichina bacteria can pass to other people in various ways. No treatment has yet been found against this bacterium so far. Statistics show that diseases caused by these bacteria are widespread.

Concerning this issue there is yet much to discover. Indeed, nowhere has the last word been uttered except in the Qur'an.

Therefore, things that are said as wisdom behind prohibiting pork are what science today has been able to explain. Maybe much more will be discovered about the harm inherent in pork in the future.

As a result, the things that were not known yesterday have been learned today, and tomorrow other things may be discovered which we are not aware of today. Therefore, instead of searching for ways to eat pork, it is better to remember that we are in a world of trials. Saying that something is prohibited because of the harm it causes is not a sound approach. Instead, it is unlawful because it is prohibited. So, even if we can eliminate the harm it causes one day, pork will continue to be unlawful. It can be argued that possible harm caused by pork can be eliminated by taking special care of the pigs and thorough medical inspection of pork. Such an argument is false, as stating that pork is harmless does not mean that it will be absolutely and completely harmless, for only the damage that can be detected with the means available at that time will be understood by people. Even if the dangers are minimized, pork will not be purified. It should also be noted that even without any reason or wisdom behind its unlawfulness, God's prohibition of it is enough to make us refrain from eating pork, all pork by-products, and/or derivatives.

MARGARINES

Whether a food item is *halal* or not depends on whether or not its ingredients are permissible. So, if a food item contains something like pork fat or any pork by-products and/or derivatives, it cannot be *halal*.

As for margarine, essence is used as an ingredient to give odor. If the essence is dissolved with alcohol, the margarine that contains it is not *halal*.

Another aspect of this issue is the fact that doctors say margarines break down at a temperature of 40 °C. The temperature of human body is 36-36.5 °C. Therefore, the body has to spend more energy to break down saturated fats, which break down at higher temperatures. Otherwise, doctors say, people will suffer from arteriosclerosis with saturated fat building up inside the capillary vessels and blocking them. To sum up, if there is nothing *haram* in the ingredients of the margarine, it can be used. But the preventative medical aspect of this issue is also important.

First of all, concerning this issue the Qur'anic verses and prophetic sayings are clear. Before slaughtering, God's name must be said. The Qur'an warns Muslims repeatedly not to eat meat of animals that are not slaughtered in the name of God.[36] This is a point neglected when slaughtering chickens. Today, chicken producers use different applications. Some of them slaughter chickens one by one by hand while others do it by machines. In both cases *Bismillah* must be pronounced. But production firms claim that it is impossible to say *Bismillah* for each chicken even when slaughtering them by hand. They claim that it is not easy to say *Bismillah* for each chicken when three chickens are cut every two seconds. Yet, books of Islamic jurisprudence write that if one forgets to say *Bismillah*, the animal is still *halal*. That is, all chickens are accepted as *halal* if, let's say, a man slaughters 100 chickens and forgets to cite *Bismillah* for some of them.

When slaughtering chickens with automatic machines, it seems technically impossible to say *Bismillah* for each chicken. For the chickens are on a moving band and are killed automatically with revolving knives. In this process there is no human factor. So, how and when can *Bismillah* be said? Actually, there is a similar issue in books of Islamic jurisprudence in sections about hunting and game animals. For instance, if a hunter shoots a flock of birds and kills more than one, all of the birds that are hit are *halal*. For, the *Bismillah* he says before he shoots the arrow is valid for all the birds in the flock. Hence, comparing the two situations, saying *Bismillah* when pushing the button of the machine will suffice for all the chickens that are to be ritually butchered until the machine stops working. Thus, instead of neglecting to say *Bismillah*, it can be said once each time the machine is started.

As for plucking the feathers of chickens, there are different applications. A prevalent application is that beheaded chickens are passed through a hot water source before their feathers are plucked. Here, two points are important: First, the heat of the water and second, whether the chickens are kept in hot water for a while or not.

The water must not be hot enough to cook chickens. Otherwise, the skin of the chickens will become loose and the dirt inside chickens will pass to other parts of them and this will make them *najis*, or impure. Therefore, the upper limit of heat must not exceed 50-55 °C. The water that is used to soften the skin of chickens should be sprayed over them. Otherwise, if they are put into a pool of water contaminated by chickens that were plucked earlier, they too will become impure. If they are tied to a band and water is sprayed over them from above and if it does not form a pool beneath them, there will be no doubts about their purity.

Because of fierce competition, firms have to take customer demands into account. Therefore, if we stand firm in what we believe to be true, things will evolve in the way we want them to be. If people believe in something and stand firm to defend it, every problem can be solved.

What are the Precautions to Be Taken for Cleanliness of Meat When Slaughtering Animals?

Edible terrestrial animals are classified into two groups: Domestic animals which can be easily obtained and slaughtered and non-domestic animals. There are some conditions for the first group to be *halal* when slaughtered. These are:

1. The animal must be slaughtered with something sharp enough that the blood will flow easily. God's Messenger told Adiyy ibn Hatim, "Shed the blood with anything you like and say Bismillah."[37]

2. For a thorough slaughtering, the trachea, both arteries on two sides and the esophagus must be cut. According to the Hanafi School, cutting these three suffice for it to be *halal*.

If an animal is heavily injured and thus needs to be slaughtered immediately or escapes so that it cannot be caught, shedding some blood of the animal is enough for slaughtering. In the time of our beloved Prophet, a camel ran away and was shot with an arrow. The Prophet consented to this incidence and ordered believers to do the same in similar cases.[38]

3. Saying the name of no one else other than God and slaughtering the animal in the name of no one but God.

4. Saying God's name while slaughtering the animal. The verses, *"So eat of meat on which God's name has been pronounced, if you have faith in His signs"* (An'am 6:118), *"Do not eat of that on which God's name has not been mentioned…"* (An'am 6:118) and the Prophetic saying, "Eat of the meat of the animals whose blood is shed and upon which the name of God has been invoked"[39] necessitate this.

    The conditions for slaughtering aim at avoiding torturing animals. The Prophet advised believers to sharpen the knife to be used in a place where the animal cannot see it and to be compassionate towards them.[40]

5. So as to be *halal*, the animal needs to be slaughtered by a Muslim or a Christian or Jew. "People of the book" are people like Christians and Jews, who were formerly sent a divine book and a prophet but forgot or distorted some parts of their religion and who do not believe the prophethood of the last Prophet, peace and blessings be upon him. These people are not accepted as being the same as those who associate partners with God and heathens. *"The food of the People of the Book is lawful unto you and yours is lawful unto them"* (Maeda 5:5). So, as long as they slaughter the animal in the name of God, their food is *halal* for Muslims and Muslims' is *halal* for them.[41] This verse has a general meaning; it includes any food except pork, wine, carrion, etc., which are *haram*.

IS IT PERMISSIBLE TO EAT AND DRINK FROM VESSELS AND UTENSILS OF NON-MUSLIMS?

Every vessel or utensil, except those made of gold or silver or plated with either of them, is permissible. This includes the vessels or utensils of "the People of the Book" and those of the polytheists. So, they are considered pure as long as one is not certain that they contain some impurity. This is because the general ruling is toward purity. God's Messenger is known to have drunk and performed ablution with water from a polytheist woman's water skin. He is also said to have eaten from vessels of "People of the Book."

Thus, eating and drinking from vessels of Jews, Christians, or even polytheists is permissible. Yet, this is only so on the condition that there is nothing Islamically forbidden in the vessel. Eating and drinking something unlawful deliberately is certainly not permissible. However, if there is something unlawful to Muslims but the Muslim is unaware of it, then eating or drinking it is lawful. One may, however, avoid eating or drinking from such vessels. For, such an act is not far from being *makruh* (abominable).

IS IT PERMISSIBLE TO ACCEPT SOMETHING OFFERED BY A NEIGHBOR ONE THINKS HAS EARNED MONEY UNLAWFULLY?

This is a problem some people encounter when visiting their neighbors and is a source doubt and distrust among neighbors. Therefore, underlining some Islamic principles that may eliminate such doubts among neighbors may prove helpful.

Some people find it difficult to accept some food or drink offered by their neighbors thinking that their earnings are not *halal*. In order to avoid such situations, they even try to constrict their relationships with their neighbors. In such cases, the relationships between religious people and their neighbors become weak and they stay away from each other. Yet, neighbors should be tolerant and respectful towards each other. Mutual respect between neighbors is very important for social relationships. Here are some principles that may regulate the relationships between neighbors:

1. Good intention is essential and Muslims should have the assumption that their neighbors' earnings are *halal*. Even if their positive assumptions are not justified, thinking in this way is better. In addition, personal or private matters should not be investigated, we should realize that suspicion is bad and will be punished by God. Therefore, good intentions should prevail among neighbors and people need not to be cautious about whether food or drink offered to them is *halal* or not.

2. A neighbor's income could truly be *haram*. In this case, a guest should intend to take from the lawful part when something is offered. Only those who earn something unlawful will be held responsible for it. Those who demand what is unlawful are responsible and will account for it before God. Therefore, they should think that some parts of the income of, for instance, a shopkeeper who sells intoxicants are *halal*. When offered some food or drink by such people, they should think that they take from the lawful part and thus continue their mutual respect and relationships.

3. A woman is not responsible for the unlawful earnings of her husband. She can spend the money earned in an unlawful way for essential needs. She can even invite guests and make offerings from the lawful part. In any case, the relationships should continue.

4. Those who are still apprehensive in such cases should buy a gift such as a book for the host or hostess and be content with an exchange of gifts or offers. This is also a practice of God's Messenger.

5. Mutual respect is essential in relationships among neighbors. Believers must never end their relationships with neighbors that are respectful and they must also be respectful towards them.[42]

The true believer follows in the footsteps of the Prophet in his dealings with all people so that they are liked and accepted by people. The Prophet said, "The believer gets along with people and they feel comfortable with him. He likes people and they like him. There is no goodness in the one who is not like this."[43]

C. CLEANLINESS OF THE ENVIRONMENT

THE SCOPE OF CLEANLINESS OF THE ENVIRONMENT

Cleanliness of the body, garments and the interiors of the house are not the only type of cleanliness. Cleanliness has a much broader application in Islam. Therefore, cleanliness of the environment should not be forgotten. For, cleanliness of the environment interests not only us as individuals, but also other people. Polluting the environment means bothering and harming other people. Yet, a Muslim should not harm other people and should not hurt any living being. Our beloved Prophet said, "Clean your courtyards" and thus advised believers to clean the surroundings of their houses as well.[44]

Polluting the environment is a despicable act, which a Muslim should not do. Islamic morals and manners prevent believers from polluting thoroughfares and places where people sit and rest. Islam does not allow people to annoy or disturb others. A Muslim should not act in an annoying way towards others.

God's Messenger saw some spit on the wall of the mosque and cleaned it himself with a piece of stone. This shows the importance he attached to the cleanliness of the environment.

Knowing that the Prophet forbade people to spit on the ground, how can a Muslim pollute the environment and disturb others? How can they annoy and harm others with their acts and conduct?

God Almighty says in the Qur'an that He loves those that are careful about cleanliness. Therefore, we should be clean and keep our environment clean so as to be among those loved by God.

Cleanliness is a state of goodness that cannot be attained with unilateral precautions. Cleanliness of the environment can be analyzed under the following subtitles:

1. Cleanliness of houses
2. Cleanliness of streets, districts, and cities
3. Cleanliness of roads
4. Providing sufficient water (because lack of water is one of the main reasons for pollution)
5. Cleanliness of the air

1. CLEANLINESS OF HOUSES AND RESIDENTIAL AREAS

The Prophet was very insistent about the cleanliness of houses and stated that angels will not enter where there is urine.[45] As reported by Aisha and Urwa ibn Zubayr, peace be upon them, the Prophet wanted Muslims to reserve a place in the house for daily prayers and to keep it clean.[46] There are also prophetic sayings which comment that the best house is the clean and spacious one, and that we should not collect filth and garbage inside the house. Umar, peace be upon him, reported, "The Prophet forbade us to perform prayers in garbage dumps, slaughterhouses, public baths, barns, and places where people pass."[47]

Parallel to these prophetic sayings, which stress the importance of the cleanliness of houses, there are many benefits of such cleanliness for health. Spacious and clean houses prevent the spread of epidemic diseases, and disposing of garbage from kitchens as soon as possible is important. Garbage provides an ideal environment for the spread of bacteria. It also attracts insects. The number and spaciousness of rooms should be enough for the family to live comfortably. Following the example of the Prophet, Muslim architects saw the courtyard as a part of the house and accepted it as the section that opens to the outside world. In a hadith about this issue the Prophet said: "A spacious house, an honest neighbor, and a comfortable mount are of a Muslim's happiness."[48] Infections are very prevalent in small and overcrowded houses. When family members live too close to each other diseases can spread more easily. Therefore, the house must be clean and large enough and garbage must not be kept inside for too long.

Every Muslim knows that when we talk about cleanliness of residential areas this includes also the physical cleanliness of places where prayers are performed. Not only is it forbidden to perform prayers in filthy places, but it is also forbidden to say God's name there. Therefore, in the letters the Prophet sent to distant tribes, he recommended that they "keep the mosques clean."[49] In a hadith, places such as garbage dumps, baths, slaughterhouses, cemeteries, and camel stables are mentioned in particular as places where it is forbidden to perform acts of worship.[50] So, cleanliness of residential areas as well as *masjids* is essential in Islam.[51] Epidemic diseases spread in crowded places very easily. As the message of Qur'an is universal, it declares that anywhere people live must be kept clean. A Muslim should avoid doing anything that may disturb others and also protect their environment. This is also a requirement for hygiene. It is well-known that all mosques and the Ka'ba, a major focal point for the pilgrimage, are kept particularly clean in keeping with the command of the Qur'an.

2. CLEANLINESS OF PUBLIC PLACES

Our beloved Prophet stressed the importance of environmental cleanliness and prohibited polluting water: "Never urinate into water. You may later need that water to perform ablution or to have *ghusl* (ritual bath). Also you must not get into stagnant water and have a ritualistic bath when you are impure after sexual intercourse. Take water with a pot and have the bath outside the pool of water."[52] God's Messenger said that he saw a woman who had been continuously cleaning the mosque in Paradise. Abdullah, son of Abbas, said: "There was a black woman called Harka. She used to clean the *Masjid al-Nabawi*. When she died the Prophet was not informed about her death. Not seeing her over the next few days, he asked about her and the companions told him of her death. Upon this he said: "When someone among you dies, inform me about it," and he performed *ghaib* prayer for her. (This is the type of prayer performed in the absence of the deceased after the funeral.) Then he said: "I saw her collecting rubbish in Paradise."[53] His concern for Umm Mihjan, who was very sensitive about the cleanliness of *Masjid al-Nabawi* is also noteworthy. She died but the Prophet was not informed about her death. When he heard about her death, he became very sad and gathered the companions to perform the prayer for her.[54]

The Prophet said: "The whole earth has been made a *masjid* and is purified for me."[55] This hadith implies that all parts of the earth must be kept clean. 'Umar's son, Abdullah narrated: "My father used to clean God's Messenger's *masjid* every Friday."[56] In another hadith, the Prophet says: "God is clean; He loves those who are clean. He is generous and he likes generosity. So keep your courtyards and open areas clean."[57] Thus, he prohibited storing garbage at home.

Picnic areas are very important for public health. Going on a picnic has become an indispensable part of people's life, especially in cities. In order to relieve the stress of the city and have a rest after a week's work, people go to the country, where there is a different and calm atmosphere. Picnic areas are chosen for their beauty, cleanliness, and silence and should not be left polluted by the visitors.

In a hadith reported in Muslim, God's Messenger says: "Be on your guard against two things which provoke cursing." They (the companions present there) said: "O Messenger of God, what are those things which provoke cursing?" He said: "Relieving oneself on the thoroughfares or under the shade where people take shelter and rest."[58] In some reports he also prohibits defecating under fruit trees.[59] As is stated by scholars who explain this hadith,[60] the prohibited place is not only the shade of fruit trees. All trees and shade under which people sit and rest are prohibited from being polluted. The shade of trees, walls, rocks, etc. is also forbidden from being polluted. This means that all public places that are known to be used by people must be kept clean. This applies not only to relieving oneself, but also to all types of pollution. In the time of the Prophet, peace and blessings be upon him, there were no glasses, cans, paper, packages, etc. So, the meaning of related Prophetic sayings includes anything that disturbs or bothers people. This is referred to as the "elimination of annoyance" and is strongly recommended. From a different perspective, these Prophetic sayings clearly show that polluting the environment with things that may harm or annoy not only people or even animals is not permissible in Islam.[61] These Prophetic sayings clearly indicate that maintaining the cleanliness of public places, roads, shady spots, and other places that are commonly used by people is among the most important things strongly recommended by Islam. Muslims must maintain cleanliness of not only their bodies, food, and drinks, but also of their environment. Muslims have a two-fold responsibility. For, both the rules for a healthy life and Islamic rules necessitate that they stay clean.

3. CLEANLINESS OF ROADS

There are many Prophetic sayings about the cleanliness of roads. The Prophet, peace and blessings be upon him, tells in detail about the wideness of roads, the construction of roads, the maintenance of their cleanliness and protecting them against highwaymen. Of these details, we will only briefly explain the ones that are concerned with our subject.

Cleanliness and protection of roads is an issue that is emphasized in particular in Prophetic sayings and is directly related to our subject. In a hadith, picking up the things from roads that may disturb people (called "elimination of annoyance" in Islamic terminology, that is anything that gives difficulty to people) is said to be "one part of faith": "The faith has over seventy branches, the most excellent of which is the declaration that there is no god but God, and the humblest of which is the removal of what is injurious from streets. Modesty is also a branch of faith."[62] This prophetic saying is included in many hadith books with slight differences of words. "Elimination of annoyance" is accepted as giving alms. In order to emphasize the importance of this kind of alms, the Prophet tells about other kinds of good deeds that have the same value as alms:

"fair conciliation between two people, helping somebody lift his load or load it onto his animal, sweet words, each step taken towards daily prayers, etc."[63]

In a hadith, God's Messenger says that a person who lifted a branch of tree from the road so that people were not disturbed and/or hurt went to Paradise because of this good deed.[64] In another Hadith, he said: "All good and bad deeds of my Umma were shown to me. Among the good deeds was elimination of what is injurious from the thoroughfares. Among the bad deeds was the spittle on the ground that was not covered with earth."[65] In another hadith reported in Muslim, a man asked God's Messenger to teach him something so that he could derive benefit from it. The Prophet said: "Remove the troublesome thing from the paths of Muslims."[66]

In the hadith mentioned above, the word "troublesome thing" is frequently used. The Prophet did not say "stone," "thorn," "filth," etc., but he said "*adha*, or troublesome thing," which comprises the meaning of all such things. This word is defined as small harm or defect in dictionaries.[67] However, from the context it is used in Prophetic sayings we understand that it stands for anything that may annoy or harm those who pass on a road.[68] It was used many times in Prophetic sayings and the Qur'an to mean "something that bothers or disturbs."[69]

4. Providing Sufficient Clean Water

Scarcity of water is one of main reasons for pollution. The World Health Organization has accepted the right to access clean and sufficient water as an essential human right: "All peoples, whatever their stage of development and their social and economic conditions, have the right to have access to drinking water in quantities and of a quality meeting their basic needs."[70]

Now, let's read the words of Prophet Muhammad, peace and blessings be upon him, who encourages the maintenance of clean drinking water 1,340 years before this conference:

"Rewards of seven kinds of good deeds reach the doer even after death, his book of good deeds does not close, rewards continue to be written for him: teaching knowledge, bringing water, digging water wells, consecrating books, and raising well-mannered children who will pray for him after his death." The Prophet clearly said that providing people with clean water will be rewarded not only in this world, but also in the Hereafter. Indeed, Muslims brought up with these commands and recommendations built water canals wherever they went. Water canals and fountains built by the great Ottoman architect Sinan form the best examples of these.

If the recommendations of the Prophet had been followed, perhaps most of the epidemic diseases in the past would not have occurred. Indeed, the World Health Organization asserts that if basic precautions concerning cleanliness had been taken, there would not have been so many epidemics. However, the rules established by Islam make a clean life possible. Islam was revealed as a religion which reshapes human life. People who live in remote places which are not very civilized do not know much about personal hygiene and the cleanliness of the environment. All people have the right to live in a clean environment. In pre-Islamic ages, people learned about cleanliness, again, from the prophets.[71]

5. CLEANLINESS OF THE AIR

Air pollution is one of the greatest problems today. Although there are many reasons for air pollution, we want to discuss only one aspect here.

When we think about the wind, we can understand that it has a very important role in cleaning the air. Indeed, it is the most effective element for eliminating air pollution. Blowing fast, it takes the polluted air away and brings fresh air, which is a source of life for every living being. This characteristic of wind is indicated in the Qur'an:

> And in the alternation of night and day, and the fact that God sends down sustenance from the sky, and revives therewith the earth after its death, and in the change of the winds, are signs for those that are wise. (Jathiya 45:5)

The term *"tasrif al-riya"* in the verse above means "blowing of the wind. The wind is also mentioned in the Qur'an as *"emissary winds, sent one after another"*[72] and *"the wind that scatters far and wide."*[73]

Ibn Haldun (1332-1406) in his *Muqaddima* speaks of the importance of ventilation and air circulation when building new cities and emphasizes the fact that roads need to be planned in the direction that the wind blows.[74]

We learn about some precautions against air pollution from Prophetic sayings. These can be summarized as follows:

a. Houses should be large.

b. Houses should not be too high.

c. Houses should have courtyards.

Air pollution is ever-increasing and it is well known that some chemicals used in some plants have harmful effects upon the atmosphere. By using such chemicals human beings are making holes in the ozone layer, which is essential for our life. This has been worrying many countries for about half a century. Even if the pollution were to stop today, it is almost impossible to undo the harm, for they have already polluted outer space. As finding solutions for air pollution is not our main subject, we deem this brief explanation to be sufficient and therefore will not go into more detail.[75]

Today, the whole world has come face to face with the tremendous problem of the pollution of water sources. Unfortunately, most of the seas are polluted today. All the creatures in these seas have been poisoned to some extent. Therefore, people feel worried about eating sea food and their suspicion is justified. The reason for all of this is the irresponsible and uncontrolled use of technology. Changing the current situation in a positive way will become possible if we make use of the laws of nature and educate people, in particular children from an early age, about the cleanliness of the environment.

CHAPTER 4

Ritual Purification

Purification of the Ritualistically Impure

In Islamic terminology, the term *hadath* is used for ritual impurities, and *tahara* is purifying from the ritual impurities which are removed either by complete ritual bathing (*ghusl*) or by ablution (*wudu'*). While the elimination of actual dirt is essential for hygiene, ritual purification from a state of impurity is necessary before the performance of such acts of worship as praying, reciting the Qur'an, etc.

What are the Types of Ritual Impurity?

There are two types of ritual impurity (*hadath*):

1. Minor impurity: This is the state of impurity that can be eliminated by performing ablution. The state of minor impurity begins, and thus invalidates ablution, because of such reasons as vomiting a mouthful of food, relieving oneself, breaking wind, and bleeding, excluding menstrual or post-natal bleeding, etc. Performing ablution is sufficient for the elimination of such states of minor impurity.

2. Major impurity: This is the state of impurity that necessitates the complete ritual bath (*ghusl*). Its causes include sexual intercourse, seminal emission, menstrual bleeding, or childbirth bleeding. Those who are ritually impure because of such causes must have a complete bath to eliminate their impurities. They cannot perform their prayers without first doing this. There is a clear command in the Qur'an, which states that menstruation is a discomfort and a state of ritual

impurity and forbids men from having sexual intercourse with their wives in such a state.[1] A woman during her menstrual or postnatal bleeding cannot perform the prayers, observe the fast, or recite the Qur'an. This is because menstruation signals ritual impurity, and thus brings about a state in which one needs to make ablution. At the end of such states, that is, when the bleeding stops, they need to have a complete ritual bath before performing the prayers. They do not need to make up the prayers they have missed while in such states of impurity, but they must make up any days of fasting they could not observe during the month of Ramadan.

To conclude, two acts to eliminate the state of ritual impurity are ablution (*wudu'*) and the ritual bath (*ghusl*). Those who cannot find water for ablution or bathing can perform dry ablution (*tayammum*). This issue will be elaborated on later in more detail.

WHAT IS ABLUTION (*WUDU'*)?

PURIFICATION AS A PREPARATION FOR DAILY PRAYERS

The daily prayers (*salat*), which include a four-level purification, are wonderful acts of worship through which we seek God's good pleasure and take refuge with Him. Through ablution or bathing to prepare for the prayers, the body and the limbs are purified from dirt and impurities.

Physical cleanliness is the first level. In a hadith reported by Abu Hurayra, God's Messenger, may peace and blessings be upon him, said:

> When a believing servant washes his face while taking ablution, every sin he contemplated with his eyes will be washed away from his face along with water, or with the last drop of water; when he washes his hands, every sin they wrought will be effaced from his hands with the water, or with the last drop of water; and when he washes his feet, every sin towards which his feet have

walked will be washed away with the water or with the last drop of water. The result is that he comes out pure from all sins."[2]

Maybe this is why God's Messenger performed separate ablution for each of the daily prayers. It is known that he never performed two daily prayers with a single ablution until the conquest of Makka.

Cleanliness of clothes and where one performs the daily prayers are the second level. This is ordained in the verse: "*And keep your clothing clean! Keep away from all pollution*" (Muddaththir 74:4-5). After passing through such a process of cleanliness, the eyes should not look at what is unlawful, the mouth should not utter obscene or bad words, the hands should not do bad things, the feet should not walk towards mischief, and thus all parts of the body should avoid sin.

The purity of the heart is the third level. Eliminating bad feelings and thoughts to earn God's good pleasure is known as "purity of the heart." God wants people to approach Him. In the Qur'an He decrees: "*Call upon Me, I will answer you*" (Ghafir 40:60). In other words, God will certainly see His servant as he prostrates before Him in daily prayers. Indeed, God says in the Qur'an, "*Remember Me, I will remember you*" (Baqara 2:152). God's Messenger says, "Remember God in your happy times so that He remembers you in your hard times."[3] This means remembering God when you are on the earth so that He remembers you in the grave, on the Day of Judgment, and on the *sirat* (the bridge across the infernal fire) when one almost loses one's footing on the bridge. This is what verses of the Qur'an and the Prophetic sayings tell us. Indeed, His servants should always seek for the ways to His good pleasure, and performing daily prayers is the best way of seeking refuge in God. Thus, believers who prepare for the daily prayers purify themselves through ablution and are ready to go into His presence. And God Almighty will be ready to accept their prayers and return them in the best way.

The last level of purification is that which was represented by the Prophets. Attained by the Prophets, this is a stage where the heart is purified from everything else but God. This is the last stage, which our Prophet and other prophets reached by passing through all previous stages. The heart cannot truly remember God without first being purified from bad manners and without saving the limbs from sins and eliminating anything related to the world. In other words, only if the inner and outer parts of the human are purified from sins can the light of faith sparkle in their heart. This means that the last stage cannot be reached without having first passed through the other stages, one by one. Just like climbing a ladder, believers will be elevated at each stage and finally find what they are looking for, and earn God's good pleasure. Prophets reached this stage in this way. For example, our beloved Prophet was very sensitive in the matter of ablution and daily prayers. He asked for forgiveness from God a hundred times a day. He said, "I seek repentance from Him a hundred times a day."[4]

By asking for His forgiveness to such an extent, even though he was a prophet and thus pure, Prophet Muhammad teaches all believers the significance of always turning to God and asking for forgiveness. Thus, believers should be in a continual process of increasing improvement and refinement.

The Prophet, who had great self-control and a pure spiritual life, prayed several times in the mornings and evenings: "O God, the Turner of the hearts, adhere our hearts to Your religion."[5] The believers should prepare for the daily prayers with similar feelings and thoughts. Preparation for such a sacred task is very important. While preparing for daily prayers and washing each of our limbs, we become exalted, renewed, and purified. Supplications that accompany the performance of ablutions bring a metaphysical dimension to this process of refinement. There are also some other supplications that are recited on the way to the mosque; these cause believers to feel that they are approaching God with every step. This door is open for most people, if not all. Some people, such as Caliph Ali, used to grow pale as if he was about to faint at the time of each prayer.[6] This shows the importance of daily prayers and hence the importance of ritually preparing for them.

ABLUTION AS BOTH PHYSICAL AND RITUAL PURIFICATION

Ablution is thorough physical purification. God's Messenger compared ablution with a river. He asserted that if believers were to bathe in that river five times a day, no filth or dirt would remain on them.[7] When believers perform ablution, they care not only about physical cleanliness but also about spiritual purity. They perform their ablution as if they were in God's presence, and they fear that they may become hypocritical if there is no balance between their inner and outer selves. The believer feels that if they clean off the physical filth but do not refine or purify their heart and thoughts, they will not be able to go into God's presence. They accept such a contradiction as impolite behavior towards God. The hadith, "God does not look to your bodies nor to your faces; He looks at your hearts"[8] is also indicative of this. If one's intentions or thoughts are not pure, that person then might be sent from the presence of God, no matter how clean they are physically. Therefore, physical cleanliness and ablution also mean spiritual purity for believers. God's Messenger informs us that ablution eradicates sins as well as ensuring physical cleanliness.[9]

In another hadith, the Prophet says, "When anyone among you wakes up from sleep, he must wash his hands three times, for he does not know where his hands have been during the night."[10] If we consult a doctor, most probably they would say that germs live mostly in damp areas such as the armpits and that millions of germs can gather under only one nail. We also know that if we touch a vessel germs will pass to the vessel and that in this way people can get infected by a variety of diseases. While sleeping, people can touch any part of their body but be unaware of it. The recommendation of God's Messenger is very important for health and cleanliness; however, we must act according to what he says not only because of the benefit to our health, but also because the Prophet has commanded us to do so. Believers perform ablution five times a day and continuously try to purify their hearts and intentions. So, both types of purification complement one another.

Ablution becomes a kind of expiation for sins and exalts believers. As soon as they put their hands under water to perform ablution, they begin to feel a deep respect for God. They stop talking and thinking about useless things. For practicing Muslims to perform their ablution with water as cold as ice on cold winter days is an awesome experience; neither heat nor cold can hinder them from performing complete ablution of the body when they need to. They carry out the Qur'anic order: *"O you who believe! When you rise up for prayer, wash your faces and your hands as far as the elbows, and wipe your heads and your feet to the ankles..."* (Maeda 5:6) and go into the presence of God in complete cleanliness. The Prophet also stated this: "Shall I tell you the things by which God obliterates the sins and elevates the ranks." His companions said, "Yes, O Messenger of God!" He said: "Performing the ablution thoroughly despite difficulties."[11] The Arabic word *asbigh* is used in the Hadith to mean "whole, complete; washing the nose and mouth thoroughly, washing hands and feet completely, etc." The term *'ala al-makarih* means to hurry to the water source to perform ablution despite all difficulties, such as cold or hot weather. The same term is also understood as "as long as it does not harm you." If there is a risk that an ill man will get worse or that his recovery will be delayed he can perform dry ablution (*tayammum*) instead of ablution with water. Similarly, if there is a high risk of becoming ill because of severe cold water, believers are free to perform dry ablution. When there is no water or when there is an impediment to using water, dry ablution is permissible as the mercy of God Almighty.

To conclude, ablution is a means of not only physical cleanliness, but also spiritual purity. Those who perform ablution as a preparation for the prayers are purified from every kind of filth and are ready to go into the presence of God.

WHAT ARE THE BENEFITS OF PERFORMING ABLUTION?

There are great purposes in all the systems God has put into the human body. Imam Ghazali says that there is nothing more perplexing than the human body. In his "Man, the Unknown," Alex Carrel writes about how fantastic the physical structure of the human body is. There are perfect systems of equilibrium and balance in the body which if changed in the slightest way will cause harm to the body.

The cardiovascular system, for example, pumps blood even to the tiniest vessels in the body throughout a lifetime and its effects are clearly visible by our pulse. This system works throughout our lives without our even knowing about it and invokes God's name at each pump. Dervishes say that *"la ilaha illa'llah"* (There is no deity but God) has the rhythm of a pumping heart. When we begin to say *"la ilaha illa'llah,"* our heart adjusts to this rhythm and begins to say *"la ilaha illa'llah"* while pumping the blood to the remotest points of our body. Just as lime scale blocks water pipes, layers of fat can block the capillary vessels, too. When they are blocked, they cannot carry blood and the organs or limbs that are far away from the heart, such as the tips of fingers, and most importantly the brain, suffer. In order for such organs to be healthy, blood circulation should function well in the body. Ablution helps the blood circulation system to function well by stimulating capillary vessels. This is very important for the circulatory system, for, when they are stimulated they absorb blood and become cleansed. The blood returns to the heart, is refined and pumped to the vessels again. This circulatory system is continuously repeated to maintain our life without our even knowing it. All these are blessings from God. At the end of the verse which mandates ablution, God Almighty says: *"God does not desire to put on you any difficulty, but He wishes to purify you and that He may complete His favor on you, so that you may be grateful"* (Maeda 5:6). What, then, is the blessing mentioned in the verse that God wants to complete? Everything given by God is a blessing. Completion of these blessings is dependent on the free will of human beings. For, the first creation is compulsory; that is God created and guided us without our knowing it. The continuity of these blessings is left to man's own free will. Doctors recommend that we should wash our limbs sometimes with hot water and sometimes with cold water to maintain the flexibility of blood vessels. Hot water helps them open and cold water makes them shrink. Performing ablution helps maintain the closing and opening of the vessels at our own free will. It is well-known that this system is also an important factor in healing injuries and protecting the body against germs. It has been written in many Islamic books of medicine that the stimulation of the lymph system is possible only by taking water into the nose or by wiping both sides of the neck with water, as is done when performing ablution. This is just one benefit of ablution. There is a static balance of electricity inside the body. The continuity of this balance is very important in maintaining the health of the body. The balance of electricity must be maintained. In particular psychosomatic diseases put the body under pressure and affect it. For example, diseases such as ulcers can be caused by such influences. Today, there are many factors which may influence the psychology of human beings and upset the electrical balance. Polluted air, synthetic clothes and receptacles are some of the factors that may harm the electrical balance inside the body and cause human beings to become unstable. Water and earth are the two most important and effective elements to eliminate this imbalance and establish a new balance. These two elements are conductive. Ablution or ritual purification with earth when there is no water regulates the electricity inside the body and discharges excess electricity. This is emphasized in the Qur'an as, "Perform ablution when you get up for the prayers, have a complete bath when you are ritually impure, perform dry ablution if you cannot find water." God is thus completing His blessings over human beings.

Islam is the religion of ease and facility. God does not want to put His servants into difficulty. As is stated in the Qur'an, *"God desires ease for you, and He does not desire for you difficulty"* (Baqara 2:185). Therefore, Islam is not a difficulty or a burden. God Almighty wants to complete His blessings for us and prayers are an important means to continue these blessings.

What is the Wisdom behind Ablution?

Ablution is not only a means of physical cleanliness. It also has deep inner meanings.

In order to perform ablution, believers make their intention, wash their hands and arms, including the elbows, wash their face from the top of the forehead to the chin and as far as each ear and clean their mouth and nostrils with water. They wipe at least one-quarter of the head, neck and ears with their hands. Finally, they wash their feet up to the ankles thoroughly. What might be the meaning of this series of established acts to clean the parts of the body in this way?

Ablution is both a physical and spiritual preparation for daily prayers, which is a means of going into God's presence. Ablution or complete ablution of the body (*ghusl*) is a prerequisite for daily prayers. Certainly, cleaning the private parts and hands after using the toilet and performing ablution cleanses the body, but physical cleanliness is not the entire wisdom. Ablution purifies believers from spiritual filth, as well. Through performing ablution believers repent for past sins and plan to do good deeds in the future and hence their penitence and regrets about past actions will help to purify them from sins. There may be times when we did not safeguard our limbs from sins or when we committed bad deeds with our bodily parts, thereby exceeding the bounds set by God.

While performing ablution, we can get rid of the negative effects of bad deeds through silent prayer. A person who wants to perform the prayers first declares their intention. This is a spiritual preparation and making an intention to go into the presence of God Almighty. Then they say: *Bismillahir-Rahmanir-Rahim* (in the name of God, the All-Merciful, the All-Compassionate) and asking God for refuge, begin to perform the ablution. Then, while they cleanse their mouth and nose, they may pray: "O my Lord! Help me to recite Your name and Your Book. Take away the smell of hell and make me feel the sweet smell of heaven." The believer can invoke the following while washing their face, "Oh Lord! Let my face shine on the doomsday when your beloved servants' faces shine. Do not let my face be darkened on that day." Washing their right arm, they may say, "O my Lord! Make me one of those who receive their book from the right. Make my account before You easy." Washing their left arm they may say, "O my Lord! Do not make me one of those who receive their book from the left." Wiping their head they can say, "O God! May Your benevolence and abundance envelop me. Let me rest under the shade of Your throne, where there is the shade of nobody but You." When wiping their ears they think, "O my Lord! Make me one of those who understand and who follow the best of words, and let me hear the voice that will invite to heaven." While wiping their neck they hope, "My Lord! Protect me against the fire of hell; do not let me do anything for which I might feel ashamed." When washing their feet they may say, "O my Lord! Cause my feet to be firm on the straight path; do not let me stray from Your path."[12]

Then the believer recites the *shahada* and supplicates further: "O God! I may have done wrong; for humans are ignorant and torment themselves. But I repent and turn to You. Forgive me; accept my repentance. For, you are the One who forgives those who repent. Make me one of those who repent and purify themselves; one of the good and righteous. Make me one of those who feel thankful, patient, and who invoke Your name."

A person who performs ablution sincerely confesses their wrongdoings and mistakes. Thus, they purify themselves and go into the presence of God asking for the acceptance of their prayers. Only then are they purified and ready to go into God's presence; that is, to begin performing the prayers.

Believers wash off the filth and impurities from their hands, arms, face, mouth, nose, and feet, that is all the parts that have contact with outer world, with water. More importantly, they accept physical cleansing and supplications as a symbol of purification from spiritual filth and dirt. Just as water cleans physical filth, so too, does repentance purify spiritual impurities. Believers should purify and cleanse not only their body and clothes, but also their hearts and thoughts, which are accepted by God as being more important. In fact, these two types of cleanliness are hardly separable for true believers.

Daily prayers are not valid without physical cleanliness; similarly knowing God is not possible without purity of the heart. The body is cleansed with water. As for cleanliness of the heart, a sincere and pure faith in the Oneness of God is necessary. Believers care for both types of cleanliness. They believe that there are protective angels on the left and on the right.[13] Those who begin a spiritual journey towards God must have both inner and outer cleanliness. Outer cleanliness is attained with water and inner cleanliness is attained with repentance and asking for forgiveness.

If a person goes into the presence of their king or president, surely they will have a bath and wear clean clothes. Therefore, when believers go into the presence of their Creator, they must purify and cleanse themselves. A believer who is content with only physical cleanliness resembles someone who paints the walls of their house on the outside but does not paint the inside before inviting a king to visit. As Shamsaddin of Sivas said, "The Sultan does not enter the place before it becomes purified and refined." Bayazid Bistami says: "Whenever I think of the world, I perform ablution, and whenever I think of the Hereafter, I take complete ablution."

Scholars of discernment speak of five ranks of ablution and purification. Beginning from the inner part to the outer parts, these five ranks are as follows:

1. Ablution of the soul: This is purifying the soul from both animal-like ignorance and obliviousness of seeing things other than God. Those who succeed in this improve their ability to know God better. If the soul is purified from all things but God, the light of *Ghaffar*, The All-Forgiving, will envelope them. If they purify their bad thoughts, they attain piety and righteousness. If they overcome the tricks of the carnal soul, that is, if they succeed in not being trapped by these, they will attain a sense of tranquility and contentment.

2. Ablution of the *sirr* (lit. "secret"): Here, *sirr* means the spiritual center or the soul of the soul. Its ablution entails purification from hypocrisy, needs and desires, conceit, ambition, excessive love of worldly things, and ambition to attain higher positions. When the impurity of the *sirr*, that is hypocrisy and love for the worldly, are washed away, the light of *ikhlas* (sincerity) becomes evident as the believer performs acts of worship as if in the presence of God. Love of worldly things is replaced by a Divine love if the greed and avarice inside the heart is cleansed and the light of contentment and resignation becomes visible.

3. Ablution of the heart: This means refraining from hypocrisy, defeatism, and bad manners. When haughtiness is washed away, modesty replaces it. When the impurity of jealousy is warded off, goodness becomes visible and when enmity is washed away, love of God becomes apparent. When treachery is washed away, betrayal and disloyalty are replaced by reliability and trust.

4. Ablution of the tongue: This means refraining from lies, backbiting, slandering, useless words, and searching for sins and secrets of other people. If lies and backbiting are washed away, they are replaced by honesty and loyalty. If slander is washed away, love becomes visible. Useful things and the name of God replace talk about useless things. If the habit of searching for other people's secrets is abandoned, the light of tolerance begins to sparkle.

5. Physical ablution: This simply means washing the parts of the body that need to be cleansed for valid ablution. Some of its results are that washing the face for ablution will make the face sparkle on the Day of Judgment. Washing the arms will lead to generosity. It will also bring about the blessing of taking the book of deeds from the right-hand side. Washing the feet will give the opportunity to pass spiritual obstacles in the other world easily. This kind of cleanliness and ablution helps believers approach nearer to God.

To complement physical cleanliness with spiritual purification believers are advised to ward off love for the world from the heart while washing the hands. When cleansing the mouth, believers should decide not to talk about useless things. When the face is washed, they should promise not turn their face towards anything other than God. When washing the feet, they should enforce their intention not to depart from the right path.[14]

Ablution is a preparation for turning towards God. Those who want proximity with God must aim to perform spiritual and physical ablution. For those who only care about what is visible, physical cleanliness is sufficient. However, those who want to earn God's good pleasure and forgiveness should also purify their heart. As physical impurity is eliminated with water, spiritual impurity is erased by repenting and ever-turning to God.

The Prophet said, "Anger is from Satan; Satan was created from fire. Fire can only be extinguished with water. So, when you get angry, perform ablution to overcome it."[15] A deep wisdom about both the physiological and spiritual merits of ablution is hidden in this hadith.

WHAT IS THE REWARD IN THE HEREAFTER FOR ABLUTION?

Performing one's daily prayers is the essence of servitude to God. Ablution is preparation for daily prayers, and physical and spiritual purity is the key. For ablution refines the soul and makes it receptive to the blessings of God. For example, when cold water flows over our body we feel tension and alertness; this is a natural result of the water. Similarly, a refined and empowered soul attains the capacity to receive blessings that come from God.

In the Hereafter, Muslims will be called by a special name because they performed ablution in the world. Abu Hurayra washed his arms almost up to his shoulders and his feet up to his knees and said, "I heard the Prophet saying, 'When my *umma* is called on Doomsday, they come with the traces of ablution like radiant light and whoever can increase the area of his radiance should do so.'"[16] In another report, he narrates the incidence in more detail:

> The Messenger of God, peace and blessings be upon him, came to the graveyard of Baqi al-Gharqad and said: "Peace be upon you all, the abode of the believing people! We, if God so wills,

are about to join you. I love to see my brothers." They (the
Companions) said: "Aren't we your brothers O Messenger of
God?" He said: "You are my companions, and our brothers are
those who have, so far, not come into the world." They said:
"O Messenger of God, how would you recognize those persons
of your umma who have not yet been born?" He said: "Suppose
that a man has horses with white blazes on their foreheads and
legs and these are among horses which were all black, tell me,
would he not recognize his own horses?" They said: "Certainly,
he would, O Messenger of God!" He said: "They will come
with white faces and arms and legs owing to ablution, and I will
arrive at the Cistern before them. Some people will be driven
away from my Cistern as the stray camel is driven away. I will
call out. 'Come! Come!' Then it will be said: 'These people
went astray from your path,' and I will say: "Be off, be off!"[17]

What is more, a hadith reported by Uqba ibn 'Amr indicates
that ablution is the beginning of a journey that will end in Heaven:

> We were entrusted with the task of tending the camels. When
> it was my turn I returned in the evening after grazing them in
> the pastures and I found God's Messenger, peace and blessings
> be upon him, standing and addressing the people. I heard these
> words: "If any Muslim performs ablution well, and then stands
> and prays two rak'ah of prayer, setting about them with his heart
> as well as his face, Paradise is guaranteed for him." I said: "What
> a fine thing is this!" A man who was in front of me said: "The
> first was even better than this." When I looked, I saw that it
> was 'Umar, who said: "I see that you have just come. Before you
> arrived, the Prophet said, 'If anyone amongst you performs the
> ablution and then completes the ablution well and then says: I
> testify that there is no deity but God and that Muhammad is
> the servant of God and His Messenger, the eight gates of
> Paradise will be opened for him and he may enter by whichev-
> er of them he wishes.'[18]

In these Prophetic sayings, the importance of a thorough ablution is emphasized and it is indicated that the Prophet will recognize his *umma* from the mark of ablution on their face and limbs
on the Day of Judgment.

WHAT ARE THE OBLIGATORY ACTS OF ABLUTION?

In order for cleanliness to be accepted as ablution, it should have some obligatory acts. These obligatory acts are stated in the Qur'an: *"O you who believe! When you rise up for prayer, wash your face and your hands as far as the elbows, and wipe your head and your feet to the ankles"* (Maeda 5:6). As is stated in the verse, ablution consists of four obligatory acts:

- Washing the face from the top of the forehead to the chin and as far as each ear,
- Washing the hands and arms up to the elbows,
- Wiping at least a quarter of the head with wet hands,
- Washing the feet up to the ankles.

According to other Schools of Islamic jurisprudence, the obligatory acts are more than four. For example, according to the Shafii School, making the intention and washing the parts of body in the prescribed order are also obligatory acts of ablution. Scholars of the Maliki School are of the opinion that intention and rubbing the parts that are washed are also obligatory. For the followers of the Hanbali School, it is also compulsory that one makes the intention and does all the acts of ablution in succession and without any delay between the acts so that a limb washed earlier does not dry out while washing the following limb.

WHAT IS WIPING WITH WET HANDS?

Literally, *masah* means wiping something with wet hands. In Islamic terminology, it means wiping the head or indoor boots with wet hands. While wiping at least a quarter of the head is an obligatory act of ablution, wiping boots that are worn indoors is permissible. In addition, bandages on any part of the body can also be wiped with moist hands in this way when making ablution (*wudu'*) or complete bath (*ghusl*) so that that part of the body becomes ritually clean. The significant point here is that the hands are moistened separately for each limb to be wiped this way so that the moisture of the hand wiping the limb is not used to wipe something else. For example, after washing the arms, the remaining wetness on the hand cannot be used to wipe the head as it has been used to wash the arms. The hand must be wet again before wiping the head.

WHAT ARE THE SUNNA ACTS OF ABLUTION?

It is sunna to perform the following acts of ablution:

- Making the intention to perform ablution (*wudu'*),
- Reciting "*Bismillahir-Rahmanir-Rahim*" (i.e., in the Name of God, the All-Merciful, the All-Compassionate),
- Washing hands up to the wrists,
- Using *miswak* or brushing the teeth,
- Taking water into the mouth and nostrils and cleansing them thoroughly,
- Saturating one's thick beard by combing it from beneath with wet fingers.
- Rubbing between fingers while cleansing hands,
- Wiping the whole head from the forehead to the back of the head at once with both hands moistened,
- Wiping the back and sides of the neck, including the ear holes and the outer ears,
- Doing each act in proper order,
- Beginning with the right when washing arms and feet and washing each limb three times,
- Performing acts of ablution without any interruptions in between[19]

WHAT ARE THE MANNERS OF ABLUTION?

In addition to the obligatory and sunna acts of ablution, there are certain manners (*adab*) that make the ablution more perfect. While performing ablution, believers can decide for themselves what they should do and what they should avoid to make a better ablution. The following are the manners of ablution:

- Turning in the direction of *qibla*, if possible, while performing the ablution,
- Not splashing the ablution water on one's body or clothes,
- Not talking about worldly affairs, but reciting prayers,
- Using water economically,
- Pronouncing the *shahada* when the ablution is completed,
- Performing two *rak'at* of supererogatory prayer after performing the ablution, if it is not a prohibited time of day for daily prayers.

What Things Nullify Ablution?

The following acts nullify ablution:

- Whatever emits from the private parts (front or back): bowel movements, urine, wind, *wadi* (a thick white secretion discharged after urination), *mazi* (a white sticky fluid that flows from the sexual organs when thinking about sexual intercourse or during foreplay, and so on), and prostatic fluid. However, semen as well as menstrual and postnatal blood require complete bath (*ghusl*).
- Emission of blood, pus, or yellow matter from a wound, blister, or pimple to such an extent that it flows beyond the mouth of the wound. If this emission is as large as the head of a pin and does not flow then it does not nullify ablution, and wiping it with the hands does not affect the ablution. Water flowing from blisters on the skin is treated as blood. Some scholars say that such water does not nullify ablution. Those with diseases such as chickenpox and infected rashes can follow this view. According to Shafii School, blood flowing from any part of the body other than the private parts does not nullify ablution.
- Vomiting a mouthful of matter.

- Loss of consciousness because of fainting, drowsiness, temporary insanity, hysteria, intoxication, and so on.
- Falling asleep while lying on one's side or sleeping while leaning against something. However, falling asleep while sitting upright does not nullify ablution because it is not the sleep itself that breaks ablution, but the possibility that as a result of sleeping one's limb may have become so relaxed that that may have allowed wind to escape. In brief, it is the state of not controlling one's body during sleep that nullifies ablution. One would, however, perform ablution after waking up from sleep in any case. This is more in accordance with the principle of avoiding doubtful things.
- Audible laughter during the prayer. This nullifies both the prayer and the ablution.
- Physical contact for pleasure between man and woman without any obstacle or with a thin barrier like a thin piece of clothing through which one can feel the sensation. However, if the head of one's penis disappears into a woman's vagina, ritual bathing is required.
- If something like a piece of cotton is placed inside the vagina and taken out when it gets wet. However, ablution is not nullified if it is not taken out so long as it does not pass wetness to its outer surface.
- Elimination of an excuse. Someone who has performed dry ablution (*tayammum*) must perform ablution when they find water. Similarly, someone who has wiped on their indoor boots must perform ablution when the period that this is allowed is complete. People who are not traveling can wear the boots for a whole day, while travelers can wear them for three consecutive days without removing their feet to wash.

DOES CRYING NULLIFY ABLUTION?

No matter what the reason is, crying does not nullify ablution. In fact, if it is because of some divine or religious thoughts, it is desirable and certainly does not harm ablution or the prayers. However, crying during the daily prayers stemming from worldly worries and distress nullifies the prayer.

The heart-felt prayer of the righteous is a means of ascension towards God Almighty. God orders us to search for ways towards Him: *"O you who believe! Be careful of God and seek means of nearness to Him and strive hard in His way that you may be successful"* (Maeda 5:35). The Prophet says that eyes which shed tears will not see hell-fire.[20] God's Messenger used to cry while performing the prayers. He used to sob and shed tears during the prayers. It is also reported that 'Umar's sobs were usually heard by those performing prayers in the back rows. God Almighty states in the Qur'an that the Prophet Jacob cried much while petitioning: *"I only complain of my grief and sorrow to God, and I know from God what you do not know"* (Yusuf 12:86).

HOW IS ABLUTION PERFORMED?

Following the obligatory and sunna acts of ablution as well as the principles of good manners (*adab*), the best method of ablution is performed in succession and is as follows:

- Stand in a position so as not to splash the ablution water on one's body and clothes and turn in the direction of the *qibla* if possible.
- Recite *"Bismillahir-Rahmanir-Rahim"* after making the intention to perform ablution and then wash hands together with wrists three times, rubbing between the fingers thoroughly.
- Remove anything fastened to the skin, such as paint, glue, adhesives, gum, etc. Cleanse the teeth with *miswak* or a toothbrush, or the fingers of the right hand.
- Cup water in the right hand and wash the mouth three times.
- Take water from one's cupped right hand into the nostrils three times and squeeze it out with the left.
- Wash the face three times with both hands from the top of the forehead to (and including) the chin and from ear to

ear. Those with beards should saturate the beard by combing it with wet fingers. As there is no need to wash the surface of the eye, those who wear lenses need not take them
out while performing ablution. As for eyebrows and mustaches, wetting them is sufficient. The skin under them
does not need to be washed during ablution. However, it
must be washed when having a ritual bath (*ghusl*).

- Wash first your right and then left arm up the elbow three
  times.

- Wipe at least a quarter of your head once with wet hand,
  or even better wipe the whole head from the forehead to
  the back of the head at once with both hands, which is the
  practice of the Prophet.

- Wipe the entrance to the ears with either the forefingers or
  little fingers and the outer ears with the thumbs, and then
  wipe the back and sides of the neck with the back of both
  hands.

- Wash first the right then the left foot up to the ankles, rubbing between the toes.

- Pronounce the *shahada* when ablution is completed. It is
  also among the manners of ablution to drink some water
  and recite the short chapter of *Al-Qadr* from the Qur'an.[21]

WHY DID ABU HURAYRA EXAGGERATE HIS PERFORMANCE OF ABLUTION?

Having heard the Prophet saying, "I will recognize my *umma* by
their parts of body they wash for ablution" Abu Hurayra was very
fastidious about ablution. He used to wash his arms up to his
shoulders and his feet and legs up to his knees. In the Hadith, the
term used for the radiance of those parts of body washed for ablution is "*ghurran muhajjalin*," meaning "pure white foreheads." Abu
Hurayra induces from this hadith that he should wash more of his
limbs. Indeed, Abu Hurayra wanted to perform a perfect ablution,
as emphasized in the hadith:

The Messenger of God said, "Shall I indicate you to something by which God obliterates the sins and elevates the ranks?" The Companions said, "Yes, O Messenger of God." He said, "Performing the ablution thoroughly despite difficulties, walking further to the mosque, and waiting for the next prayer after observing a prayer; that is mindfulness."[22]

WHAT ARE THE TYPES OF ABLUTION?

There are three types of ablution:

1. Obligatory (*fard*) ablution: Ablution for any of the prayers is obligatory by Divine decree. Without ablution, one cannot perform the prayers, whether they be prescribed daily prayers or sunna, or supererogatory prayers, nor should a person touch the Qur'an.

2. Necessary (*wajib*) ablution: Ablution is necessary for those who want to circumambulate the Ka'ba. Although circumambulating the Ka'ba without ablution is valid (excluding the states when one needs to have *ghusl*, or full ablution), this should be expiated by sacrificing an animal or giving alms, depending on the type of circumambulation.

3. Recommended (*mandub*) ablution: There are many states in and occasions on which ablution is recommended. The following are some of the occasions where performing ablution is accepted as a good deed:

   - Performing ablution out of respect when holding and reading religious books, such as those of Islamic law, hadith and Islamic faith. Scholars were very careful about such issues. Imam Hulwani, for instance said, "I attained the knowledge as a result of my respect for knowledge. For, I have never touched even a piece of paper without first performing ablution." Similarly, Sarahsi, one of the great Islamic jurists, once said when he had diarrhea, "I had to refresh my ablution seventeen times during the night in order to continue my studies."
   - Before going to bed

- After waking up
- To be continuously ritually purified
- To refresh ablution
- After accidental sins, such as slandering, backbiting, telling lies, swearing, etc.
- After laughing loudly
- To eliminate anger. God's Messenger is reported to have said, "Anger is from Satan; Satan was created from fire. Fire can only be extinguished with water. So, when you are angry, perform ablution to overcome it."[23]
- To recite the Qur'an by heart, although the Qur'an can be recited this way silently, without taking ablution.
- To study or explain Prophetic sayings
- To learn or teach a religious subject
- To stand at Wakfa in Arafat and when walking between Safa and Marwa
- To eliminate doubt in certain situations which are said to nullify the ablution in certain Islamic schools
- To wash the dead and attend a funeral procession.

WHAT IS THE ABLUTION OF THE EXCUSED?

This is a principle of Islam that facilitates and eliminates difficulty and hardship. There are states that would normally nullify ablution, like the flow of blood; however, if they are partially permanent, they are accepted as excuse. Thus, those who have this excuse are allowed to perform acts of worship in such states as a continually bleeding nose or wound, being unable to control urine, or women's continuous bleeding, etc. Physical ailments that go on during the time of a daily prayer are accepted as excuse, as well.

People who have certain excuses should perform ablution for each of the five daily prayers. They can wait to perform daily prayers until the end of the time for each prayer. When the time of the next prayer begins, they should perform ablution again. In addition, as the ablution they made for dawn prayers is nullified by the sunrise (the end of the time for that prayer), they must perform a separate ablution for midmorning or 'Eid prayers. Another important issue is that such people cannot lead congregational prayers.

WHAT ARE THE BENEFITS OF BEING IN A CONTINUOUS STATE OF ABLUTION?

One should do righteous deeds as much as possible. A continuous state of ablution is a righteous deed, and it is recommended. However, excess even in positive actions is not permitted. Facility and doing the things that can be easily done is essential. Nobody should take responsibility for what they cannot do. Believers must do those things that are obligatory. As for other recommended deeds, they should do these as much as they can. In a hadith the repeated performance of ablution is called a "light upon light." The Prophet used to perform separate ablutions for each of the daily prayers. He would immediately perform ablution whenever the call to prayer was heard. His companions reported that he only performed one or two prayers with a single ablution at the time of the conquest of Makka. This shows that he used to perform ablution even when he did not need to; he also performed ablution before going to bed. He indicated this in one of the hadiths, "Before going to bed, perform ablution. Enter your bed, put your hand under your head and turn to the *qibla*, and say a prayer. If you die, you will be a martyr."

HOW DOES ONE WIPE INDOOR BOOTS OR BANDAGES?

Once ablution has been performed it is permissible to pray wearing indoor boots which will be wiped during the ablution; these boots will be worn for a whole day for those who are not traveling and for three consecutive days for travelers. It is known that the Prophet wiped over his *khuffayn*.[24] *Khuffayn* are a type of footwear, like indoor boots, or a soft leather footwear. Wiping these with at least three fingers of a wet hand is called *masah*. Conditions for the *masah* are as follows:

1. Those who wear indoor boots must put them on after washing their feet during ablution.
2. Indoor boots must be close-fitting, covering the foot up to the ankles and the feet should not easily come out of them.
3. They must not be of flimsy material (durable for at least six kilometers).
4. They must not absorb or pass water to the feet.
5. There must not be any large holes in them.[25]

If one wishes to wear indoor boots over a bandaged foot, they should first wipe over the bandage and then wear the boot. It is also permissible to wipe any cloth or bandages that are wrapped around any wounded limb if it would be harmful to open the bandage. Ablution performed in this way is accepted as valid and these limbs are considered as having received ablution. If even wiping is harmful then it can be omitted all together. Wrapping the bandage without first performing ablution or in a state of ritual impurity is not an obstacle for wiping with wet hands. There is no allotted duration for wiping of this kind, either. Changing the bandage does not invalidate the wiping, thus it does not need to be done again. It is nullified with the healing of the wound.

WHAT NULLIFIES THE WIPING OF INDOOR BOOTS?

Everything that nullifies ablution also nullifies the wiping with wet hands. However, the feet are not washed when performing ablution if the indoor boots have not been taken off, as long as the duration for wiping is not over yet. But, taking them off, either unknowingly or on purpose, nullifies the wiping, thus the feet must be washed during the ablution. If the ablution has not been nullified when the indoor boots are taken off, then it is sufficient to wash only the feet for the prayers. Similarly, being in a state of ritual impurity because of seminal emission, menstruation, or childbirth bleeding nullifies the wiping.

WHAT IS RITUAL BATHING (*GHUSL*)?

Ghusl is the act of washing the entire body with clean water. It is ordained upon Muslims in the following verse: *"If you are in a state of ritual impurity, bathe your whole body"* (Maeda 5:6). *Ghusl* purifies both the actual and ritual impurity that result from seminal emissions, menstruation, or childbirth bleeding. Women should take a bath at the end of menstruation; marital relations are forbidden during menstruation and before women are purified by ritual bathing (Baqara 2:222). The traditions of the Prophet provide detailed explanations about purification from menstruation and childbirth bleeding.

Having a bath refreshes the body, eliminating the tiredness and lethargy one experiences in such states of ritual impurity as marital relations, wet dreams, etc. and brings about a new balance in the body. It also regulates the blood circulation and prepares believers for the atmosphere of worship. It has many other benefits for both physical and spiritual health.

WHAT OCCASIONS NECESSITATES RITUAL BATHING?

1. Sexual Relations and Wet Dreams

Among the secretions of semen, *mazi*, and *wadi* which emit from the sexual organs, only semen necessitates complete bathing. *Mazi* is a white sticky fluid that flows from the sexual organs when thinking about sexual intercourse, foreplay, and so on. *Wadi*, on the other hand, is a thick white cloudy secretion, which has no smell, discharged after urination and occasionally before. Though the secretion of *mazi* and *wadi* do not necessitate complete bathing (*ghusl*), they do nullify ablution (*wudu'*) and need to be washed off before refreshing ablution.

Both men and women become ritually impure, and thus bathing is required if the head of the penis disappears into the vagina, even if there is no discharge of semen or orgasm. Here, the emission of semen is the second cause of ritual impurity. Excretion of semen during sleep also makes bathing obligatory. Therefore, if one sees a mark of semen on underwear after getting up in the morning, this necessitates bathing, even if no dream can be remembered. However, bathing is not required if there is no mark of semen on the underwear or body, even if the dream is remembered. So, any seminal emission caused by lust necessitates ritual bath. If semen comes out because of lifting something heavy, falling or any illness, it does not require ritual bathing.

2. Menstruation and Childbirth Bleeding

Bathing is obligatory upon the completion of the monthly menstrual period and childbirth bleeding. Bleeding after the completion of such periods is accepted as excusable and thus does not necessitate ritual bathing.

Regulations concerning the state of being ritually impure are the same as those concerning menses and post-childbirth bleeding. However, women are prohibited from sexual intercourse during such periods. Women in such states cannot observe the fast or perform the prayers. While a woman must make up the obligatory fasting days after regaining her ritual cleanliness, she does not make up any prayers she has missed during menses.

WHAT ARE THE TYPES OF RITUAL BATHING?

There are three types of ritual bathing:

Obligatory (*fard*) bathing: Complete bathing is obligatory for the purification of ritual impurity resulting from sexual intercourse, wet dreams, menses, and post childbirth bleeding. In addition, washing the corpses of Muslims is a communal obligation (*fard al-kifaya*) for Muslims. This is an indication of respect for human beings, and the respect and love for those who have lived as Muslims. Martyrs, however, are buried without being washed.

Sunna bathing: Having a ritualistic bath for Friday prayer is the practice of the Prophet. As is stated in Prophetic sayings, Friday is the noblest of the days, and the day of assembly on which Friday prayer is performed in congregation at mosque. It is the holy day for Muslims. Considering numerous Prophetic sayings concerning bathing on Fridays, scholars have concluded that having a bath on Friday is "*Sunna mu'akkada,*" that is, what the Prophet emphasized or enjoined in word or deed. It is also recommended that general personal hygiene be carried out on Friday by cutting the nails and trimming the moustache and beard.

In addition, it is sunna to have a bath for Eid prayers and for *waqfa* at Arafat as well as before entering the *ihram* (lit. "consecration") of both minor pilgrimage (*umra*) and major pilgrimage (*hajj*). Women with menstruation or childbirth bleeding can have a bath before entering the *ihram* of pilgrimage, as this is actual but not ritual cleanliness.

Recommended (*mandub*) bathing:

- It is recommended that those who are in a state of ritual impurity should not delay in taking their baths. Although they can delay it until the time of prayers, it is better to have a bath early.

- According to the Hanafi and Shafii Schools of Islamic Jurisprudence, it is recommended that those who embrace Islam should have a bath before saying the Shahada. According to the Maliki and Hanbali Schools of Islamic Jurisprudence, however, this is necessary (*wajib*). There is a consensus among scholars that if the person who has embraced Islam is in a state of ritual impurity, having a bath is obligatory. Such bathing means being purified from all kinds of sins before accepting Islam and beginning a new clean life.

- Having a bath upon reaching the age of fifteen. A girl or a boy who is not sexually potent until the age of fifteen is legally accepted to have attained the age of puberty and it is recommended that they have a bath when they reach this age.
- Having a bath after loosing consciousness as a thanksgiving for having recovered.
- Having a bath after donating blood.
- Having a bath before washing a dead person.
- Having a bath on such holy evenings as Bara'a and Qadr.
- Having a bath while staying in Mina and Muzdalifa.
- Having a bath before going to Makka and Madina as an act of respect.
- Having a bath at the time of lunar and solar eclipses and before prayers performed solely on the occasion of lunar and solar eclipses.
- Having a bath before the ritual prayer for rain.
- Having a bath for repentance of sins.

WHAT ARE THE OBLIGATORY ACTS OF BATHING?

As is stated in the verse, *"If you are in a state of ritual impurity, bathe your whole body"* (Maeda 5:6), washing the whole body is obligatory. As the mouth and nose are accepted as parts of the outer body, they must be washed as well. Therefore, washing the whole body, as well as cleansing the mouth and the nose with water three times, are obligatory acts of ritual bathing.

WHAT ARE THE SUNNA AND MANNERS OF BATHING?

Pronouncing *Bismillah*, making the intention, and washing the hands and private parts first, then performing ablution (*wudu'*), washing and rubbing the entire body completely, not wasting water, not exposing the private parts and not talking are some of the sunna and manners of bathing.[26]

WHAT ARE THE MERITS AND BENEFITS OF BATHING?

Bathing has many spiritual aspects beyond just washing the whole body as an act of cleanliness. Ritual purification makes cleanliness and water, as a purifying agent, an inseparable part of Islamic civilization. Countless public baths in Islamic countries are only one indication of this fact. In the past, public baths and mosques were the first public structures to be built in residential areas.

The benefits of having baths for one's health are obvious. Bathing after marital relations and seminal emission makes the body renewed and relaxed. Certainly, bathing is beneficial not only for the human body, but for spiritual life, as well. The need of a spouse and family is a natural and instinctive need, which God through His Wisdom has placed in human beings. Fulfilling sexual urges is part of human nature and a means for continuing the human race. If this natural inclination is seen as the ultimate aim, the spiritual and religious dimensions of human nature will be neglected. The carnal soul will become impure while seeking the fulfillment of sexual pleasures, and it will not be interested in a spiritual life.

On the one hand, a person who is completely immersed in spiritual life will find it difficult to adapt themselves to the physical world. On the other hand, someone who is excessively indulgent in the physical world will be distracted from spiritual pursuits. Overemphasis on only the physical dimension and a disregard of the balance will lead one into error. Therefore, a human's spiritual and physical needs require regulation if there is to be success and well-being both in this life and in the Hereafter. A transition between the two domains is necessary for balance, and ablution and bathing regulate and facilitate this process.

Just as a person who has fainted is brought to by having water splashed on their face, a person who passes through a transformation process during sexual intercourse and who becomes distant to the spiritual dimension becomes themselves again when they have a bath and they are ready to return to the spiritual domain.

Commenting on the hadith, "I have been made to love three things in your world: Women, pleasant fragrance, and the Prayer, the light of my eyes,"[27] Muhyiddin ibn Arabi (1165-1240) writes:

> All creation and, in particular, the human being are a manifestation of God Almighty. Therefore, one's love for someone is, in fact, love for the One Essence. If one perceives the One this love is for, they will be aware of Who this pleasure is from. God, as the true Owner of love, is the One Who must be loved the most. As is stated in the hadith above, God makes man yearn for woman and woman for man. When they love each other, they desire union, that is, the goal of union exists in love. The physical form of this union is sexual intercourse, during which the instinct of lust encompasses the whole body. Because of this physical union during which couples become annihilated in one another's body in lust, complete ritual bathing is prescribed after intercourse.
>
> God does not want His servant to turn to anybody save Him and is very jealous of the servant who finds pleasure in other than Him. For this reason, God Almighty wants the couple to cleanse themselves of this impurity caused by an appetite for others than Him. Thus, ritual bathing becomes a means of turning to Him, Who is the Essence and Real Being. This way, the couples purify themselves of the effect of annihilation in each other in lust.[28]

Ablution and complete bathing are perfect means of cleanliness. Yet, essentially they have symbolic and ritualistic meanings. Becoming purified before going into the presence of God is the essential aim of ablution and ritual bathing. This is confirmed by the fact that ablution or ritual bathing can also be performed with earth or sand (*tayammum*) when there is no water. God's Messenger said, "God does not look at your appearance, but He looks at your heart and deeds." That is to say, the primary nature of purification is spiritual. The most important means of spiritual purification is to cry or shed tears, thereby turning to God in sincere repentance. Jalaladdin Rumi says, "Visible filth can be washed out with some water. However, the filth that piles up in the heart can be purified by nothing but tears."[29]

What is the Ruling of Having Cavities Filled While in a State of Ritual Impurity?

Cleansing the mouth with water is important, as washing the mouth during ritual bathing is obligatory according to Hanafi and Hanbali Schools, and sunna according to Shafii and Maliki Schools.[30]

Purification from a state of being ritually impure is very important for Muslims, but this has nothing to do with filled or crowned teeth, as it is the inside of the mouth and not the teeth that must be washed during bathing. Therefore, it is pointless to worry about filling teeth while in the state of ritual impurity, as it is not an obligation to wash inside the teeth but the outside of the teeth.

What Acts of Worship are Unlawful for Those Who are in a State of Ritual Impurity?

Performing the following acts of worship is unlawful (*haram*) for those who are in a state of ritual impurity:

1. Performing the prayers and reading the Qur'an, even if it is only one verse. However, reciting verses of thanksgiving and supplication only with the intention of remembrance of God (*dhikr*) and supplication (*dua*) is permissible. Thus, it is permissible, in fact recommended, for women who are in a state of ritual impurity during menses or childbirth bleeding to pray, to ask for God's forgiveness, and make remembrance of God. So, menstruating women can recite *Fatiha*, the opening chapter of the Qur'an as a supplication. It is also permissible for a person in such a state to pronounce the *Kalima Shahada*: "*Ashhadu an la ilaha illa'llah wa ashadu anna Muhammadan Rasulul'llah*" (I bear witness that there is no deity but God, and I bear witness that Muhammad is God's Messenger) or "*Subhana'llah*" (glory be to God) for *tasbih*, or "*Allahu akbar*" (God is the Greatest) for *takbir*. Moreover, teaching the Qur'an to children word by word is permissible for a person in a state of ritual impurity. In addition, looking at the Qur'an without intending to recite

in such a state of impurity is not accepted as touching the Qur'an and is thus not forbidden.

2. Holding the Qur'an or touching its verses, even if it is only one verse or half a verse. However, the Qur'an can be held or carried within a case or covering on which no Qur'anic verse is written. Similarly, it is forbidden to hold a plate or a coin with a verse on which a verse of the Qur'an is written when in such a state of ritual impurity.

3. Circumambulating the Ka'ba and, unless necessary, entering a mosque. In case of absolute necessity, one can be in a mosque in such a state of impurity. Someone who has a wet dream inside a mosque, during retreat for instance, must perform dry ablution (*tayammum*) before leaving the mosque. However, he cannot recite the Qur'an or perform the prayers with this dry ablution.

WHAT IS THE RULING OF DELAYING BATHING WHILE BEING IN A STATE OF RITUAL IMPURITY?

When a believer is in a state of ritual impurity, they can stay in that state only until the due time of the prescribed daily prayer. Thus, the upper limit for delaying the bath is the end of the duration for daily prayer. To miss a daily prayer is unlawful (*haram*). It is better to eliminate such a state of impurity as soon as possible. In a hadith, the Prophet recommends performing ablution (*wudu'*) in such a state and retiring to bed until the time of the dawn prayer.[31] Aisha, the mother of believers, reported that after washing his hands and mouth and performing ablution (*wudu'*), the Prophet used to eat, drink, and sit in a state of ritual impurity. On another occasion, Abu Hurayra reports, "The Prophet met me in the street and at that time I was in a state of ritual impurity. So I avoided him and went to take a bath. On my return the Prophet said, 'O Abu Hurayra! Where have you been?' I answered, 'I was in a state of ritual impurity, so I disliked sitting in your company.' The Prophet said, 'Glory be to God! A believer never becomes impure.'"[32] With this, the Prophet emphasized that one can sit and talk with others in such a state. Moreover,

God's Messenger used to lean his head on the lap of his wife, Aisha or sit next to her and cover himself when she was menstruating.[33]

WHAT IS DRY ABLUTION (*TAYAMMUM*)

Tayammum literally means intending or proposing to do a thing. In Islamic terminology, it is an act of purification done with earth or the like to purify and get ready for acts of worship when there is no water or when it is not possible to use water. Dry ablution (*tayammum*) became permissible in the fifth year after Hijra. During the Bani Mustaliq Campaign in the fifth year after Hijra, God's Messenger, together with his army, passed a night in a place where there was no water. Early in the morning, they found no water to perform ablution for the dawn prayer, and the permission to use earth for this purpose was granted with the revelation:

> If you are in a state of ritual impurity, bathe your whole body. But if you are ill, or on a journey, or one of you comes from offices of nature, or you have had contact with women, and you find no water, then take for yourselves clean sand or earth, and rub therewith your faces and hands, God does not wish to place you in a difficulty, but to make you clean, and to complete His favor to you, that you may be grateful. (Maeda 5:6).

The Companions rejoiced at the revelation and performed dry ablution for the dawn prayer. Thus, the earth becomes fit for ritual purification when water cannot be obtained.

HOW IS DRY ABLUTION PERFORMED?

This purification by earth is done to get rid of impurities which occasion the need for ablution (*wudu'*) or bathing (*ghusl*), so that one is ready for performing prayers or any other act of worship that cannot be performed without ablution. Obligatory acts of dry ablution are comprised of making the intention and wiping the face and the arms. For this, one touches earth, sand, or stone lightly with both hands and wipes the face. They touch it a second time and wipe their arms up to and including the elbows.

Dry ablution is a blessing and a great facility, as God Almighty enables believers to worship even in the most difficult situations. He maintains the believers' spiritual needs and makes them look at the earth, which is the essence of their nature and they feel modesty and respect for the Creator.

WHAT ARE THE RULINGS OF DRY ABLUTION?

Dry ablution (*tayammum*) as substitution for ablution or bathing is an exceptional practice. Only when there is a legitimate excuse for dry ablution, does it become permissible and valid. These excuses can be classified into two groups:

1. Lack of water for ablution or bath. When there is no water, a person must search for it in the surrounding area before performing dry ablution. If he is in a city or any other residential area, he will most probably find water. If he is on a journey and if there is a possibility of finding water within an area of one mile (1609 meters), he must go and search for it. However, if it is not safe to go that far, this is a viable excuse and he can perform dry ablution. It is not compulsory to go and look for a source of water further than one mile.

2. Presence of an obstacle for using water. Dry ablution is allowable when water cannot be used because of some religiously viable reasons. If there is a possibility of becoming ill or of an illness getting worse or if a doctor, preferably a Muslim one, says that water is harmful to a certain disease or wound, it is permissible to perform dry ablution. According to the Maliki School, if a specialist Muslim doctor cannot be found, the advice of a non-Muslim specialist doctor can be used in such cases.

WHEN IS DRY ABLUTION PERFORMED?

Dry ablution is allowable for those who have legitimate excuses under the following circumstances:

- If there is danger for one's life, property, or something in one's trust because of using water
- If the water found is not sufficient for ablution or bathing
- Existence of a strong possibility that a person or their companion or their animal will die of thirst if the available water is used for ablution or bathing
- When there is no means of getting water, even if there is water. For example, when there is no rope or bucket to pull water from a well
- When water is sufficient only to wash out actual filth
- The possibility of missing an irreplaceable prayer, such as that of a funeral or 'Eid Prayer. Purification by sand is allowable when the time needed to have ablution or bath would cause one to miss such an irreplaceable prayer; but this dispensation does not apply to the Friday Prayer or to the prescribed daily prayers which can be made up before the expiry of the time for the prayer. It is important that if there is a possibility of being in time for such an irreplaceable prayer or if it is known that the congregation will wait, dry ablution (*tayammum*) is not permissible. In this case, ablution becomes obligatory.

WHAT ARE THE CONDITIONS OF DRY ABLUTION?

It is essential to make the intention for dry ablution. The reasons for dry ablution and the conditions for it being obligatory are the same as those for ablution (*wudu'*). However, one must perform a separate dry ablution for each occasion that necessitates ablution. Thus, the intention for dry ablution to perform prayers, or any other acts of worship that cannot be done without ablution must first be declared. While starting dry ablution, it is a must that a separate dry ablution be preformed for each act of worship, even if they are performed one after the other. For instance, if someone who is in a state of impurity that necessitates bathing has to enter the mosque, he performs dry ablution with the intention of entering the mosque; however, he cannot perform prayers with the same dry ablution.

To perform dry ablution, palms of both hands must touch soil, sand, stone or the like. The whole face and arms up to the elbow must be rubbed. Things such as rings and bracelets must be taken off or moved in order to wipe the skin underneath them.

If someone is handicapped and cannot use water, he can perform dry ablution by rubbing his face and arms with earth. Such a person, after making the intention, can get help from others who will rub his arms and face with earth. Someone whose hands or arms are amputated may perform dry ablution by rubbing only their face against the earth. If such a person has a wound on their face, they may perform prayers without dry ablution.

WHAT IS THE SUNNA OF DRY ABLUTION?

The following is a description of how dry ablution is performed in accordance with the sunna:

1. Pronounce "*Bismillah*" and make the intention before commencement.
2. While keeping the fingers wide open, move the hands forwards and then backwards when placed upon the earth.
3. Shake off the soil from the hands and then wipe the entire face, using both hands.
4. Strike the earth again in the same way, and rub the right and then left arms alternately from the fingertips, up to and including the elbows.
5. Perform all these acts without interruption, in this order.

WHAT THINGS ARE ACCEPTABLE FOR DRY ABLUTION?

Dry ablution can be performed with a pure earthy substance, such as soil, sand, gravel, gypsum, a lump of clay, salt deposits, etc. Similarly, any form of stone, such as marble, tile, brick, ruby, emerald, or coral can also be used. Dry ablution is also valid if the hands are wiped over something that has been mixed with earth, with salt or even on walls that are plastered with mud. It is not important whether these things are covered with dust or not.

It is unlawful to do dry ablution with wood, grass or with wood ash, nor with elements that can be melted or molded such as iron, gold, silver, or glass. In addition, tanned skin with the fur on, fabric, or clothes cannot be used for dry ablution, as these are not earthy substances. However, if there is some visible dust on such things, the hands can be rubbed on the dust for dry ablution.

WHAT THINGS NULLIFY DRY ABLUTION?

The things that nullify ablution (*wudu'*) as well as those that occasion the need for bathing (*ghusl*) nullify dry ablution. Dry ablution performed because of such legitimate excuses as danger, illness, severe cold, etc., is nullified when such an excuse disappears. Similarly, if someone who has performed dry ablution sees water while performing the prayer their dry ablution is nullified.[34] The end of the time for the prayer also nullifies the dry ablution; i.e. if one takes dry ablution for the dawn prayer, the sunrise nullifies the ablution.

MENSTRUAL, POSTNATAL, AND NON-MENSTRUAL VAGINAL BLEEDING

WHAT IS MENSTRUATION?

Menstruation is the natural periodic discharge of a mixture of blood and tissue from the reproductive organs of sexually mature females. Menstruation happens once a month from puberty until menopause, unless a woman is pregnant or ill. Though at what age menstruation begins depends on physical characteristics, genetics, environmental, and climatic conditions, it generally starts between the ages of 11 to 13 and continues until the age of 45 to 50.

The blood flow usually lasts from three days to 10 days each month. It is reported that the Prophet said, "Menstrual discharge is at least 3 days and at most 10 days."[35] If it is less than 3 days or more than 10 days, it is accepted as non-menstrual vaginal bleeding. The duration in which women are ritualistically clean continues for at least 15 days between two menstrual cycles.

Sexual intercourse with menstruating women is, as stated in the Qur'an, unlawful.[36] Moreover, in line with the teachings of the Prophet, prayers missed during menstruation are not expiated, while fasting days not observed during menstruation are to be made up later.[37] The fact that women do not read the Qur'an or perform certain acts of worship is an exemption and facility for them.

WHY IS PERSONAL HYGIENE AND HEALTH CARE IMPORTANT DURING MENSTRUATION?

Understanding the way the menstrual cycle works each month is an important step in improving reproductive health. Menstruation is part of a cycle that helps the body prepare for the possibility of pregnancy each month. This is a natural physiological process during which an egg cell is released from the ovaries and sent to the uterus once during a menstrual cycle, which lasts on average four weeks. If the egg that is sent to the uterus is fertilized by a sperm cell, it attaches itself to the wall of uterus where it slowly develops into a baby. If it is not, it is shed together with the thickened lining of the uterus during the menstrual cycle. Then, the inside of the womb is restored and prepared again for releasing eggs from the ovaries. Until a woman reaches menopause, this cycle happens every month with great precision, except if she is pregnant or unwell. This automatic renewal of the lining of the womb for another ovulation is an exceptional preparation for the creation of a fetus. This process, which seems a burden for women, is in fact necessary for their health and a preparation for the creation of a new life.

During menstruation, women may have various kinds of problems, including menstrual pains, abdominal pains, headaches, or emotional sensitivity. They may feel depressed or easily irritated because of the rising and falling hormone levels. In addition, a suitable environment for germs occurs as blood vessels widen during bleeding. Recent studies about the lymph system inside and around the womb clearly show that any neglect concerning hygiene or personal health care can lead to many serious diseases. Catching cold during this period can lead to serious illnesses.

If women start bleeding more heavily or less than what is normal, or experience bad pains, or any other problems, they should consult a doctor immediately. Taking a warm bath usually lowers menstrual pain and cramps. As the body is weak during this period and thus can easily catch a cold, women with menses should avoid cleansing with cold water. Young girls should be trained about cleanliness during their periods, as careless cleansing of private parts may spread and thus increase activities of germs.

Precautions concerning the protection of the uterine wall must not be underestimated, as the slightest external influence, such as catching cold or sexual intercourse during menses, can greatly harm the epithelium of the uterus. The uterine wall is very susceptible and vulnerable during menstruation, a time at which blood vessels widen. This is like touching an open wound or doing a surgical operation without washing one's hands. Even if men and women carry no diseases, there may be germs on their private parts. As women are more at risk during bleeding, they should avoid sexual relations that may cause dangerous diseases or inflammation. If a woman already has an ovarian infection, this can spread or become worse. In addition, mucosa erosion inside the womb is closely related with sexual intercourse that occurs before the menstruation period is completely over. In brief, sexual intercourse during menstruation is very harmful, especially for women, and its negative consequences may continue for years.[38]

WHAT IS CHILDBIRTH BLEEDING?

There is no lower limit for childbirth bleeding, but the upper limit is forty days. Acts of worship, such as daily prayers or fasting, are performed after childbirth bleeding ends. If the bleeding does not stop after forty days, the bleeding is then treated as an excuse. In such cases, all acts of worship are performed as if the woman was in a state of ritual purity, except that ablution is performed before every prayer.

What is Non-Menstrual Vaginal Bleeding?

Non-menstrual bleeding is a continuous vaginal bleeding. Like the bleeding of nose or any other limb, non-menstrual bleeding nullifies ablution. As described by God's Messenger, it is caused by fissures in the vessels and leads to continuous bleeding until this situation is remedied.[39] There were 3 or 5 women who were known to have such an ailment during the time of the Prophet. One of them was Zaynab b. Jahsh, one of the wives of God's Messenger. The Prophet advised her thus: "Take a bath when you get up for the dawn prayer. Take a bath again shortly before afternoon prayer and perform the midday prayer and the afternoon prayer with that. Towards the end of the time for the evening prayer, take another bath and perform the evening prayer and the night prayer." Thus, bathing is performed three times during the day and none of the daily prayers are missed. God's Messenger also added, "If you can, do like this. Otherwise, perform ablution for each prayer."[40]

Women with such an excuse can choose either of the two ways, for both have been recommended by God's Messenger. Obviously, the first choice is more virtuous; but this can be rather difficult. One can also follow the second choice in line with the principle of facility and easiness, which is inherent in the essence of Islam.

What are the Rulings Concerning Menstruation, Childbirth Bleeding and Non-Menstrual Bleeding?

Islam is a religion of facility. Menstruating women are not responsible for any of the prayers. They do not perform prayers during menstruation and childbirth bleeding, and women who are undergoing these states do not make up for the prayers they missed. Since menstruating women miss many prayers over several days during their period, it would be a great burden for them to expiate the missed prayers. As for childbirth bleeding, women do not perform acts of worship during this period. Such a restriction during childbirth bleeding is to be regarded as a mercy and relief as expiating missed prayers for 20 or 30 days or even 40 days would be a great burden for women. Therefore, Islam, which is a blessing for the universe, has excused women from the responsibility of performing prayers on such days.

- Remembrance of God (*dhikr*), invoking the *tahlil* of *"la ilaha illa'llah"* (There is no deity but God), calls of God's blessings and peace upon the Messenger and his family, or any kind of supplications (*dua*) are permissible for women in such states of ritual impurity, although it is unlawful for them to perform prayers. Moreover, menstruating women can perform ablution and invoke God, turning to the direction of the Qibla in a sitting posture at the time of each prayer so that they will not miss the pleasure of prayers. In this way, they demonstrate their willingness to perform prayers if it was not for their state of ritual impurity. It is reported that the women who have done this will attain the greatest reward of prayers.

- Observing the fast is not permissible, either. However, unlike the prayers, women must make up for the missed days of fasting when they leave such states. As fasting is observed only once a year, it is not very difficult to expiate a few missed days. This is why women take on the responsibility for expiating the missed days of fasting.

- It is also not lawful to read the Qur'an. Concerning this God's Messenger said:

  "Those in a state menstruation or ritual impurity after seminal emission and marital relations cannot read any part of the Qur'an." However, people in such states are allowed to recite supplications, the prayers of praise and glorification, etc. Although it is not permissible to read the Qur'an, such people are allowed to listen to it. In addition, it is unlawful to touch the Qur'an, a verse, or even some words of the Qur'an in such a state of impurity.

- A female teacher of the Qur'an should get her assistant to teach the Qur'an while in a state of ritual impurity. According to Hanafi scholars Karhi and Tahawi, they should go on with their teaching. Tahawi says she can teach half a verse at a time. According to Karhi she can teach the words one by one in a state of ritual impurity.

- Women in a state of impurity because of menstruation and childbirth bleeding cannot enter mosques if there is no absolute necessity.

- It is not permissible to circumambulate Ka'ba in a state of ritual impurity.

- During menstruation and post-childbirth bleeding sexual intercourse is also unlawful and is one of the great sins. The Qur'an says, *"And they ask you about menstruation. Say: It is a discomfort; therefore keep aloof from the women during the menstrual discharge and do not go near them until they have become clean..."* (Baqara 2:222). Aisha, the mother of believers, reported; "The Messenger of God would recline in my lap when I was menstruating, and I would comb his hair." This hadith shows that menstruating women are not accepted as dirty (*najis*). Those in a state of childbirth bleeding are also not accepted as such. This is only ritual impurity, which means that those in such a state cannot perform certain acts of worship.

- It is unlawful for the husband of a menstruating woman to touch his wife's naked body between the navel and the knees.

- Bleeding other than that of menstruation and childbirth is not an obstacle for fasting or for the prayers. It does not hinder sexual intercourse, either. However, this is a state of excuse, so acts of worship must be performed accordingly.

WHAT IS THE WISDOM BEHIND NOT PERFORMING ACTS OF WORSHIP ON SUCH DAYS OF RITUAL IMPURITY?

God is the true Owner of all things. He does as He wills. He has ordained that women are not responsible for performing acts of worship during states ritual impurity. Similarly, men are not allowed to perform acts of worship when they are in a state of impurity because of sexual intercourse or seminal discharge. It is also not permissible for them to touch the Qur'an before they perform ablution.

Women have to deal with many hardships in daily life. God has exempted them from the responsibility of performing acts of worship during menstrual and childbirth bleeding. However, women will be rewarded as if they have performed acts of worship in such periods. Certainly, this is so if they perform acts of worship when they are ritually pure. Therefore, there is no injustice here. God is the All Just and the All Merciful, and the restrictions on normal activity during such periods are, indeed, a mercy and a relief.

SUCKLING BABIES DURING A PERIOD OF RITUAL IMPURITY

Some women assert that they never suckle their baby without performing ablution first. Although this is advisable, it is not a decree of Islam. However, it is not altogether without purpose. It is a kind of righteous behavior, which may bring about abundance.[41]

Islam is the religion of ease and facility and nobody has the right to make it difficult. Therefore, women can suckle their babies without performing ablution during such periods, provided that they wash their hands and the tip of their breasts. When the period is over, it is recommended that they perform ablution before suckling their babies. This may bring about abundance and blessings for the baby.

Throughout Islamic history, many great scholars and jurists have been brought up by mothers who have been very careful and sensitive about such practices. Seyyid Hüseyin Arvasi, who was a teacher of Said Nursi, once asked his mother, "How did you bring up your children to be so intelligent?" Nuriye Hanım answered: "I never missed *tahajjud* prayer (a supererogatory prayer performed waking up at night) except during times of ritual impurity, and I never suckled them without performing ablution first." Therefore, it is recommended for those who want to bring up their children to enlighten humankind in the future to follow the steps of such righteous and virtuous mothers.

CHAPTER 5

Spiritual Cleanliness and Purity

PURITY OF HEART

WHAT IS TO BE UNDERSTOOD BY "PURITY OF THE HEART"?

The term *saleem*, in Arabic is used to mean a "pure, sound" heart. The word Islam is derived from the same root as this word. *Qalb al-saleem*, as used in the Qur'an, means a heart that is not sullied by sins, or a heart that is purified with repentance and which asks for forgiveness. In a more specific context, it means a heart that is closed to everything else but Islam.

A sin becomes an invitation to other sins, as each one leads a person to another. If the sin is not washed away with repentance, the heart becomes rusty; and if this state of impurity continues, the heart dies.[1] The pure heart is also known to be the heart of those who never harm another. In a hadith God's Messenger says; "A Muslim is one from whose tongue and hand other Muslims are safe."[2] This is a perfect definition of Muslims with a pure heart, as a true Muslim urges kindness and avoids upsetting others.

It is possible to have a pure heart (*qalb-al saleem*) only by living in accordance with the Qur'an, which has been sent to all humanity via His last Messenger to arrange their life. This includes all good deeds. God's Messenger led a perfect life guided by the Qur'an. Once Sa'd ibn Hisham asked Aisha, may God be pleased with her, about the character of the Prophet. She replied: "Don't you read the Qur'an?" He said, "Yes." Then she said: "His character is the Qur'an."[3] His *umma* must take his example and arrange their life according to his teachings.

A pure heart is the heart which is free of all kinds of unbelief, hypocrisy, distrust, and from the association of partners with God. The heart of someone in disbelief can never be completely pure, no matter how kind the person is. These days, there are people who say, "My heart is pure for I love people; I try to be helpful to them." These are useless words as such a person can never become purified unless they believe in God. Someone who denies the Lord of the Worlds cannot be righteous or just. Of course, respect for the values of humanity is very important. However, full appreciation of such values and the continuity of this appreciation depends on faith. Without faith, all beauty and good deeds are either deceptive or temporary. It is not possible to purify the heart by separating faith and good deeds from one another, as they complement each other.

In the worldly system a defiant person who does not respect but rebels against a just head of state is punished, despite any good deeds or services they may have rendered to their country and fellow countrymen. Their good deeds will be of no use in saving them from this end. Similarly, a person who denies God or associates partners with Him, no matter how much they benefit others, will be punished in the Hereafter, and their good deeds will be of no use to him. Therefore, the heart, first of all, must be purified from unbelief, hypocrisy, and associating partners with God.

Secondly, the heart must be adorned with the principles and manners of Muslim life as prescribed in the Qur'an. Only such a heart is purified. If it is not refined, purified, and aligned with the principles of Islam, it cannot be accepted as pure.

God Almighty decreed to Prophet David: "Keep that home empty for Me so I will be in it."[4] Some have interpreted "keeping the heart empty" to mean purifying the heart from all that is not God, and not having relations with others without considering God's pleasure first. This can only be achieved by those who seclude themselves from others while living among people at the same time. Since the purpose of seclusion is to purify the heart of love that is not directed toward God and to be always with the Beloved, those who always feel the presence of God while living among people and who continuously discern the Divine Unity amidst multiplicity are regarded as always being with God in seclusion. In contrast, however, others who, although they spend their lives in seclusion, have not purified their hearts from attachment to whatever is other than God, have deceived themselves and all their attempts are futile.[5]

God's Messenger says, "When a person commits a sin, a black spot forms in his heart. If he regrets it and repents for it, his heart shines again."[6] We learn from this Hadith that the "pure heart" is the heart that has not corroded, but rather one that has been purified from sins by asking for God's forgiveness with sincere repentance.

WHAT ARE THE SIGNS OF A PURE HEART?

Purity of heart depends upon following the way of the Prophet. God says to His Prophet Muhammad:

> Say, O Muhammad: "My Prayer, and all my acts and forms of devotion and worship, and my living and my dying are for God alone, the Lord of the Worlds. He has no partners; thus have I been commanded, and I am the first and foremost of the Muslims (who have submitted to Him exclusively)." (An'am 8:162-3)

So, the sign of a pure heart is to love the Messenger, obey his orders, and abstain from whatever he forbade; also God should be worshipped in the manner that the Prophet demonstrated, said, did, or approved of. Therefore, the more a person adopts the exemplary life of the Prophet, the purer their heart will be.

Following the example of the Prophet, believers should strive to secure other people's happiness both in this world and in the Hereafter. Living for others or dedicating their life to the cause of making other people happy is one of the main characteristics of believers. If people try to achieve this with pure faith instead of running after the satisfaction of their own ego, even the hearts that are rusted will be washed clean.

The Qur'an depicts the people who are saved on the Day of Judgment as follows: *"The Day when neither wealth will be of any use, nor offspring, but only he (will prosper) who comes before God with a sound heart"* (Shu'ara 26:88-9). Thus, everything our hearts have inclined to in this world other than God is but an adornment of the life of this world alone, and it is purity of heart that will save believers in the Hereafter, not their wealth or numerous children.

One's faith is reflected in their manner of life and their outward aspect, including in particular their faces. When God's Messenger said that he will recognize his *umma* (followers) when everybody is summoned on the Day of Judgment, he was asked how he would distinguish the believers. The Prophet said: "Just as you recognize a white-footed horse with a white mark on its face from among horses which are pure black, I will recognize my *umma* from the traces of ablution." This means that God's Messenger will recognize his followers from their bright faces and white limbs because of ablution on the Day of Judgment.

Abu Hurayra used to wash his arms up to his shoulders when performing ablution. When asked why he did so, he said, "Because I want to increase the brightness of my limbs."[7] The believers will be distinguished from other communities on that Day not only by the virtue of the light shining from their faces, hands, and feet because of their habit of performing ablution, but also from the marks of prostration on their forehead as attested in the following verse: *"...Their marks are on their faces, traced by prostration"* (Fath 48:29). Faith requires believers to do what is ordained by God and His Messenger. And all the things believers are required to do are ordained for the purpose of purifying the hearts of believers.

An act of worship such as the daily prayer, which has both physical and spiritual aspects, cannot be performed without both spiritual and physical cleanliness. Daily prayers protect believers against all bad things. The soul, intellect, and heart are all exalted through fasting. Observing the fast makes a person obedient to God and purifies them both physically and spiritually. Prescribed alms purify wealth and relieve the conscience. *Hajj* (pilgrimage) erases vanity and makes one as pure as the day they were born. Is it possible to purify the heart without doing these acts of worship? Certainly not. Therefore, the most explicit sign of the purity of heart is the performance of acts of worship.

WHAT SHOULD BE DONE TO ATTAIN PURITY OF THE HEART?

It is an obligation incumbent upon every human being to recognize the diseases of the heart as well as what causes them so that the heart can be liberated from these diseases. Some of the vices and weaknesses to be purified from the heart are as follows:

- *Hasad* (Envy and malice): This means desiring the nonexistence of some of the blessings God has given to someone else.
- Hatred: Having feelings of enmity, hate, and vexation. Such feelings cause further jealousy and enmity.
- Vanity: This means taking excessive pride in oneself and thinking that one is superior to other people.
- Meanness: This means being stingy and unwilling to spend for others.
- Self-conceit: This means the arrogance one feels for some achievements in the fields of, say, science or good deeds.
- *Riya* (Pompousness): This is displaying self-importance and showing off so that others appreciate one.
- The desire for fame: This temperament blocks the path to righteousness and has been condemned.
- Boastfulness: Taking pride in one's race or ancestors. This is also a habit that is condemned and prohibited.
- Anger: Flying into a rage with the desire for revenge.
- Backbiting: Talking about some characteristics of a person who is not present and who would not be pleased if they heard what was talked. Talking about the physical body, behavior, words, religion, habits, clothes, etc of another person are all examples of backbiting.

- Gossiping and sedition: This is the act of promoting dissent and enmity among people through gossip.
- Telling lies: Saying something that is not true in a conscious effort to deceive is one of the major sins.
- Talking too much: This is also a condemned behavior. For, it leads to many other sins, such as talking about or promoting sins and gossiping about people.
- There are also some other bad behavior and manners, like false belief, committing sins, neglecting repentance, ignorance of performing acts of worship, cheating, setting traps, treachery, greed, gluttony, desiring to commit sins, listening to futile things, not trying to prevent atrocities and wickedness, cursing, spreading slander about fornication, swearing, giving false testimony and false oaths, making fun of others, belittling people, rancor, brawling, harming people, conceit, oppression, extravagance, excessive jokes, commotion, fondness of ornamental display and luxury, desire for sin, negligence, hoarding wealth, shamelessness, cowardice and so on.

The heart will be pure as long as it is purified from such vices and weaknesses. One cannot claim that their heart is pure unless they strive to cleanse their selves of all that is bad or evil.

Purifying the heart can be accomplished by adorning it with good manners such as a sound faith, decisive repentance, refraining from committing sins and regretting past sins or shames, servitude to God, patience, modesty, contentment with what has been bestowed by God, gratitude, thankfulness and glorification of God, truthfulness, loyalty, trustfulness, fidelity, complying with the rights of neighbors, generosity, greeting people, doing one's job in the best way, longing for the Hereafter and renouncing the world, considering the world to be worthless and insignificant, worrying about giving an account before God in the Hereafter, being modest, being compassionate towards living beings, perseverance against hardships, longing for God's pleasure, staying away from those who are not mindful of God, continuously thinking that God is present everywhere, refraining from things that give excessive worldly pleasures, being in a state of fear and hope, generosity, forgiveness, affection, helpfulness, consoling those in grief, understanding, preference of others' interests over one's own, counsel, leading a virtuous and chaste life, submission to God, resignation, courage, bravery, love of God, the desire to reach Him and the fear of leaving Him, politeness, doing one's job carefully and not in haste, accounting for one's carnal soul, being just, desiring goodness for others, fighting continuously against Satan and the carnal soul, refraining from useless arguments, remembering death, controlling the desire to live long, learning the Qur'an in detail, avoiding bad thoughts, not letting anything abide in the heart other than God, knowing that God is the One to take refuge in, and being sincere under all conditions.[8]

In fact, each of these virtues and good manners involves great truths. Believers can purify their heart as long as they resist the temptations of the carnal self and bad behavior and set such laudable moral qualities as guides for themselves.

A LUCID EXAMPLE OF A HEART PURE OF DECEPTION AND JEALOUSY

Anas ibn Malik narrated: "One day we were sitting with the Prophet. Some time later, he said: 'Now one of the people of Paradise will come." One of the *Ansar* (Helpers) came. Drops of ablution water were dripping from his beard. He was holding his shoes in his left hand. The following day, God's Messenger said the same words and again the same man came.

On the third day, when God's Messenger left the congregation and the group dispersed, Abdullah ibn Amr ibn As followed the man and said: "I argued with my father and vowed not to go home for three days. Can you accept me as a guest during this time?" The man accepted.

Abdullah later told us: "I stayed for three nights at the man's house. He did not get up for nightly prayers even once. He slept until the time of dawn prayer. He just said the name of God and glorified God when turning over in bed. I did not hear him say any bad words. When three nights had passed, I told him: "I did not argue with my father. On three consecutive days God's Messenger said, 'Now one of the people of Paradise will come,' and each time you came. I wanted to be your guest to see the good deeds you do and do them myself. Indeed, I did not observe any great acts of worship. How did you attain the rank that God's Messenger told us about?"

The man said: "I do not have any acts of worship other than what you have seen." When I left him and set off on the way, he called from behind: "I told the truth. I have no other acts of worship. But, I do not have any feelings of dishonesty, hatred, malice, or jealousy towards Muslims." I said, 'This is what made you attain that rank.'"[9]

CLEANLINESS OF INCOME AND EARNINGS

Cleanliness of income and earnings means that these things are "*halal*," which is a Qur'anic term meaning lawful, legal, permitted, or allowed. According to Islam, only what is *halal* can be consumed. That is, anything that is consumed must be religiously lawful and clean.

Muslims cannot simply consume anything they desire. Consumption must be for the purpose of improving their souls and their senses. Consumption has aspects that also pertain to the Hereafter. Believers should take into account the negative aspects of the things they consume both in this world and the Hereafter and refrain from anything harmful. In this way they earn and consume within the limits set by Islam. Anything they earn or consume must be lawful and clean. For, the Qur'an says: *"O humankind! Eat of that which is lawful and wholesome in the earth, and follow not the footsteps of the devil. Surely, he is a manifest enemy for you"* (Baqara 2:168). In many other verses, God advises believers to eat of the things He created as sustenance and not to follow Satan. Satan is the greatest enemy of God. In another verse, this issue is explained more explicitly: *"O you who believe! Eat of the good things that We have provided you with, and give thanks to God if you are of His servants"* (Baqara 2:172).

One mindful of and thankful to God must eat and drink from that which God has created to be lawful and clean. The following verse further emphasizes the issue and underlines what has been ordained by God:

> Forbidden to you is that which dies of itself, and blood, and flesh of swine, and that on which any other name than that of God has been invoked, and the strangled animal and that beaten to death, and that killed by a fall and that killed by being smitten with the horn, and that which wild beasts have eaten, except what you slaughter, and what is sacrificed on stones set up for idols and that you divide by the arrows; that is a transgression. (Maeda 5:3)

Some communities may accept these to be lawful and consume them. However, God does not let His servants, whom He created with a clean and pure nature, eat things that are not pure. This is why Islam follows the principle that *"Corrupt women are for corrupt men, and corrupt men are for corrupt women, just as good, pure women are for good, pure men, and good, pure men are for good, pure women"* (Nur 24:26) and prohibits anything impure for believers. Cleanliness is a very fundamental issue in Islam. This is why God's Messenger says, "Cleanliness is half of faith."[10]

Now, let's take a closer look at the cleanliness and purity of the things we consume. In Islam, the sphere of forbidden things is very small, while that of permissible things is vast. And things that are consumed, as was mentioned earlier, must be lawful and clean. Therefore, for instance, alcoholic drinks are not accepted as a consumable beverage. They are called *"rijs"* in the Qur'an, which means that they are filthy and impure both physically and ritualistically. Whatever intoxicates is unlawful and strictly prohibited. Islam does not accept them as possessions. Therefore, if someone spills, for instance, alcoholic drinks onto the ground, they do not have to pay for it, for according to Islamic law, this is not something that has any worth or value. The Messenger forbade trading in intoxicants, even with non-Muslims.

All that God has created and the benefits derived from them are permissible for humanity to use. In the Qur'an, God always decrees lawful means of work and lawful earnings. All economic activities are permitted in Islam, provided that they do not harm the community's interests or violate Islamic laws or values. Nothing is unlawful except what is forbidden by a sound and explicit Qur'anic verse or a clear, authentic, and explicit *sunna* (practice or saying) of the Prophet. Interest, usury, black marketeering, bribery, speculations, and publishing misleading advertisements are all forbidden in Islam.

Different communities now encourage and promote the use of beer "with no alcohol" and legalize the selling of soft drugs so that hard drugs can be kept under control; this is as the Prophet forewarned: "A group of people will make intoxication lawful by giving it other names" and "A time will come when people will devour usury, calling it 'trade.'" Just as Islam forbids whatever leads toward the unlawful, it forbids resorting to technical legalities in order to do what is unlawful by devious means or excuses.

WHAT ARE THE OBJECTIVES OF INCOME AND EARNINGS?

The virtuous ways of earnings can be graded as follows:

A. The most virtuous aim of earning money is to spend it on God's way or to block all avenues leading to what is unlawful in order to eliminate anything between God and His servants in its broadest context and meaning.

As one of the significant ways of spending in God's cause, *zakat* (the prescribed purifying alms) is simply spending what has been bestowed by God for the sole purpose of physical and spiritual purification in the amount and places designated by Him:

> Prescribed Purifying Alms are meant only for the poor and the destitute (albeit, out of self-respect, they do not give the impression that they are in need), and those in charge of collecting (and administering) them, and those whose hearts are to be

won over (for support of God's cause, including those whose
hostility is to be prevented), and to free those in bondage (slav-
ery and captivity), and to help those overburdened with debt
and in God's cause (to exalt God's word, to provide for the war-
riors and students, and to help the pilgrims), and for the way-
farer (in need of help). This is an ordinance from God. God is
All-Knowing, All-Wise. (Tawba 9:60)

The ultimate goal is to elevate the poor in order to turn them,
in time, into *zakat*-givers themselves. Moreover, *zakat* eliminates
meanness and purifies possessions. *Zakat* also makes the rich more
compassionate and tenderhearted. *Zakat* prevents poor people from
becoming jealous of or feeling hostile towards the rich. It empow-
ers a sense of brotherhood and unity.

B. Islam encourages Muslims to engage in profitable trade and
perceives this as an important source of income. The following are
just a few among the numerous Prophetic sayings that encourage
trade: "On the Day of Judgment, the trustworthy and honest merchant will be resurrected with the Prophets, the righteous and the
martyrs."[11] "The honest merchant will be resurrected under the shade
of God's Throne on that day (the Doomsday) when there is no
shade."[12] "Nine-tenths of sustenance is in trade."[13]

C. Agriculture and handicrafts are very important in Islam.
Obviously, sustenance procured through handwork or great effort
is recommended and encouraged by God and His Messenger: "*Say:
Work, and God will see your work, and so will His Messenger and the
true believers*" (Tawba 9:105).

Once God's Messenger went somewhere outside Medina on
some business. On his way back to Medina, he saw a man who was
working in his garden. The Prophet approached him and held the
hand of the man who was hoeing. While rubbing the hoer's chapped
hand to his blessed face, he said: "The hands that deserve God's
pleasure are these hands." The man who was hoeing was very happy to learn from the Prophet himself how esteemed his job was. By
rubbing the man's hand against his face, God's Messenger showed
the importance he gave to all workers and laborers.

The principles of earning or making a profit via any of such ways are as follows:

1. It is an obligation incumbent upon every Muslim to earn at least enough to meet the basic needs of themselves and their family. In a hadith, the Prophet says, "God loves the believer who earns his living with the labor of his hands."[14] This means that God both loves and appreciates believers who are skillful and capable. In another hadith, the Prophet says, "Nobody has ever eaten a better meal than that which one has earned by working with one's own hands."[15] Yes, indeed, anything one earns with personal effort is the most favorable provision.

2. Earning more than this to spend for the destitute, as well as helping relatives is recommended.

3. It is permissible to earn enough to lead a prosperous, comfortable life. When Muslims perform a permissible action with a good intention, the action becomes an act of worship, so long as both the aim and the means chosen to attain it are honorable and pure.

4. Even if the means of income and earning is lawful, the goal of outperforming others for earning praise, wantonness, or excessive living is abominable and impermissible.[16]

What are the Impure and Unlawful Income Sources and Earnings?

Islam orders all kinds of transaction or dealings to be free from unlawful means of earning. The following are some major unlawful ways of making a living that are prohibited in Islam:

a. Interest

Interest is condemned and prohibited in the strongest possible terms in the Qur'an and the Sunna. The Qur'anic injunction about the unlawfulness of interest is crystal clear, as it is amongst the prohibitions which all dealings and transactions must be free from:

> As to those who devour interest, (even though they seem, for a time, to be making a profit), they turn out like one whom Satan has bewitched and confounded by his touch, (and they will rise up from their graves in the same way before God). That is because they say interest is just like trading, whereas God has made trading lawful, and interest unlawful. To whomever an instruction comes from his Lord, and he desists (from interest), he may keep his past gains (legally), and his affair is committed to God (– if he repents sincerely and never again reverts to taking interest, he may hope that God will forgive him). But whoever reverts to it (by judging it to be lawful), they are companions of the Fire, they will abide therein. God deprives interest (which is thought to increase wealth) of any blessing, and blights it, but makes alms-giving (which is thought to decrease wealth) productive. God does not love any obstinate unbeliever (who regards what God has made lawful as unlawful or vice versa), any obstinate sinner. (Baqara 2:275–6)

As is explicitly stated in the following verses, the Qur'an is extremely strict about interest, so much so that regarding it as lawful amounts to persistence in unbelief and sin, and still taking interest, although regarding it as unlawful, amounts to rebelling against God and His Messenger:

> O you who believe! Keep from disobedience to God and try to attain piety in due reverence for Him, and give up what remains (due to you) from interest, if you are (in truth) believers. If you do not (and you persist in taking interest, whether regarding it as lawful or not) be warned of war from God and His Messenger. If you sincerely repent (and give up all interest transactions completely), you will have your principal. Then you will neither be doing wrong nor being wronged. (Baqara 2:278–9)

Dependence on interest not only discourages people from working but also destroys social solidarity. It discourages people from doing good to one another and from lending out of good will.

Concerning interest, God's Messenger tells of four types of people who are cursed: "God condemns the devourer of interest, its giver, its scribe, and its bystander. They are all equal in the dealing of sin."[17] Indeed, Islam wishes to block all the ways that lead to the exploitation intrinsic in this parasitical practice.

b. Gambling

Islam prohibits gambling in all forms, including, but not limited to internet gambling outfits, casinos, games that involve betting, such as horse or dog racing, and lotteries, regardless of whether they are run by governments or not. It is forbidden in Islam to seek relaxation and recreation in or to acquire money by gambling. In addition, lotteries and raffles organized in the name of "charitable institutions" or "humanitarian causes" are absolutely forbidden in Islam.

The Qur'an calls gambling the filth of Satan and teaches us that it is akin to drinking, idolatry, and divining by arrows:

> O you who believe! Intoxicants and games of chance and stones set up and arrows are only uncleanness, the Satan's work; shun it so that you may be successful. The Satan only desires to cause enmity and hatred to spring in among you by means of intoxicants and games of chance, and to keep you off from the remembrance of God and from the Prayer. Will you then desist?" (Maeda 5:90-1)

Any game of chance is harmful from all aspects. Gambling is harmful for both individuals and communities. It is a means of violating both the rights of God and His servants. A society where gambling is prevalent is a society misguided by Satan.

c. Trading in intoxicants

Islam has strictly prohibited any trade in intoxicants, even with non-Muslims. In a Hadith, the Messenger expressed the fundamental principle that "Every intoxicant is *khamr*, and every *khamr* is prohibited." Here, *khamr* is any substance that causes intoxication. Thus, any substance which befogs the mind is unlawful. This includes all kinds of alcoholic drinks and any hard or soft drugs like marijuana, heroin, cocaine, hashish, etc.

As clearly stated in another Hadith, everyone involved in the production and sales of intoxicants, including the one who consumes the intoxicants, who transports them, sells or buys them, or is an intermediary in any such dealings, or the one who benefits from the profits of selling intoxicants is condemned:

> God has cursed the one who produces intoxicants, the one for whom they are produced, the one who consumes them, the one who conveys them, the one to whom they are conveyed, the one who serves them, the one who sells them, the one who earns from their sale, the one who buys them, and the one for whom they are bought.[18]

d. Treachery in dealings and transactions

All kinds of cheating are prohibited in Islam. Any form of unjust exchange in dealings or making profit by cheating others in business transactions is prohibited. As is stated in the following hadith, he who deceives is not of the believers: "Whoever defrauds us is not one of us."[19]

A seller must inform the buyer about all the characteristics of the thing they are selling and inform the buyer about the defects, if there are any. Such a conduct will not only secure trust, but also invoke God's abundance. Honest traders will be shaded under the shade of God's Throne and will be assembled for judgment together with the righteous and martyrs on the Doomsday.

In Islam, it is not permissible for the seller to refrain from mentioning the defects of a commodity. The following tradition shows the significance given to absolute justice and fair play in business dealings: Once, when passing by a grain merchant, the Prophet thrust his hand into the heap of grains and found it wet. "What is this, O merchant?" he asked. "It is because of rain," the man replied. The

Prophet then said to him, "Why did you not put it on top so that the people could see it? He who deceives us is not of us."[20]

The Muslims of earlier times observed the practices of truthfulness in transactions and described the commodity they sold, exposing the defect in the commodity. Today, however, trade seems to be based on misleading people, often mentioning something that is not true about the commodity. In particular, TV commercials and advertisements claim the goods to be very different from what they actually are. They cheat large masses of people by making use of every trick to convince and deceive when promoting their commodity.

e. Profiteering

While freedom of trade and competition in the marketplace is guaranteed by Islam, it severely condemns hoarding in order to make a high profit or withholding the commodity from the market so that it becomes scarce. Hoarding and manipulating the prices at the expense of public interests are very strongly denounced in Islam. Hoarders' seeking speculative gains cause an artificial crisis in the economy and thus affect the whole society. Those who accumulate wealth at the cost of others have a parasitical, cruel nature that exploits people. Concerning hoarders, the Prophet said: "Those withholding goods until the price rises are sinners."[21] In another Hadith he said, "Whoever stocks a good essential for people for forty days is far from God, and God's mercy is far from him."[22]

f. Usury

The greed of the rich to earn more and more without caring about how they make their profit has always been a source of trouble for humankind. The third chapter of the Qur'an gives the following significant admonition to the believers:

> O you who believe! Do not devour usury, doubled and redoubled; and act in piety, keeping from disobedience to Him in reverence for Him, so that you may prosper (in both worlds). (Imran 3:130)

The exploitation of the poor by usurers negates tranquility and generates envy and hatred among the poor towards the rich. Throughout the modern age, the situation of rich lenders living parasitically on the poor has resulted in a struggle between capital and labor. Usury and interest have destroyed social peace, and even caused momentous events, resulting in social disorder, conflict, and at times have bred revolutions, as the modern Islamic scholar Said Nursi writes:

> The following two attitudes are the causes of all revolutions and social corruption, as well as the root of all moral failings:
> First: I do not care if others die of hunger so long as my own stomach is full.
> Second: You must bear the cost of my ease – you must work so that I may eat.
> The cure for the first attitude is the obligation of zakat (the Purifying Alms) prescribed by the Qur'an. The cure for the second attitude is the prohibition of all interest and transactions with usury. The justice of the Qur'an stands at the door of the world and turns away interest and usury, proclaiming: No! You have no right to enter. Humankind did not heed this prohibition and have suffered terrible blows in consequence. Let them heed it now to avoid still greater suffering.[23]

Instead of hoarding wealth and making the rich richer and the poor poorer through doubling and quadrupling the sum lent, in the Qur'an God Almighty says to *"lend God a good loan (by spending out of one's wealth in His cause)"* (Maeda 5:12), and thus purify the wealth. God gives the glad tidings to those who give in charity *"desiring God's pleasure, it is these who will get a recompense multiplied"* (Rum 30:39), and *"Those who spend their wealth night and day, secretly and in public, their reward is with their Lord, and they will have no fear, nor will they grieve"* (Baqara 2:274).

WHAT ARE THE CONSEQUENCES OF UNLAWFUL EARNINGS?

God has arranged the human selfhood or ego in such a way that it has inclinations towards both good and evil: *"And He Who has inspired it (the human selfhood) with the conscience of what is wrong and bad for it and what is right and good for it*" (Shams 91:7-8). God Almighty has created the selfhood not only with the power to distinguish between the two but also with a disposition to heed Divine prohibitions. Thus, the path of prosperity for human selfhood lies in choosing what is good and striving to make it prevail over evil: *"Truly he succeeds who purifies it (i.e. the human selfhood). And he fails who corrupts it*" (Shams 91:9-10).

The prime role of Islam is to help human beings obtain a "second nature," and the major portion of building the Muslim personality comes from the Islamic fundamental of "purification": *"Prosperous indeed is he who purifies himself*" (A'la 87:14). It is an important principle of Islam that a bad act can only be eliminated with a good one. God's Messenger said, "God Almighty is good and accepts only that which is good,"[24] and that "God does not eliminate an evil with wickedness."[25] Since money earned through unlawful means is unlawful, spending such money is also unlawful. If such money is given as charity, this will not be accepted from the donor by God. In fact, this very act doubles the sin rather than preserving the giver from the severity of their sin. For, the person who gives unlawful money makes a good and pure practice of Islam impure with their unlawful earnings, and there will be no blessing or abundance in money earned through such unlawful means.

Consuming even a morsel of unlawful food will suffice to erase the reward of prayers performed over forty days. This is a great loss, indeed. It is the right and duty of every person to consider not only the rights of other individuals, but also the rights of society in general. Any violation of personal or communal rights, no matter how it happens, will in fact lead to the violator perishing in the Hereafter unless they repent and pay for the private or public rights of others while in this world. God's Messenger did not perform the funeral Prayer of someone who had violated the rights of others before his death. The Islamic faith, therefore, maintains both the personal interests of individuals and the collective interests of the people as a community.

Each society holds the reins of its fate in its own hands. God does not make an honorable community despicable or an upright one disgraceful unless they change themselves with respect to their beliefs and lifestyle: *"Surely, God does not change the condition of a people unless they change what is in themselves"* (Ra'd 13:11). Thus, a society that does not care for what is lawful (*halal*) and what is forbidden (*haram*) will be far from God's mercy and compassion. Treachery in transactions, interest, usury, profiteering, gambling, theft, misleading advertisements, and trading in intoxicants are various means of violating and usurping the rights of other people. Their strict prohibition in Islam is a result of its deep concern for the spiritual, ethical, economic, and social welfare of humankind. God Almighty prohibits such unlawful, evil practices and guides His servants to prosperity in both worlds: *"And whoever purifies himself does so for the benefit of his own soul. And to God is the homecoming"* (Fatir 35:18).

The material, ritual, and spiritual aspects of cleanliness cannot be separated from each other as they complement one another. The Qur'an draws our attention to the spiritual garment of piety where it mentions bodily dress,[26] to spiritual nourishment where it mentions provision,[27] and to spiritual purity where it mentions being clean of body.[28] This is because Islam guides human beings not only in their outward behavior, including all their deeds and worships, but also teaches them how to purify their hearts and souls.

NOTES

CHAPTER 1
WHAT IS CLEANLINESS?

[1] Ibn Manzur, *Lisan al-Arab*, IV, 504-506; Jurjani, *Kitab al-Tarifat*, 93.

[2] Yazır, Elmalılı Hamdi, *Hak Dini Kur'an Dili*, VIII, 416-7.

[3] Ibn Kathir, *Tafsir,* 4:154.

[4] Muslim, *Tahara*, 1; Abu Dawud, *Salat,* 73; Tirmidhi, *Tahara,* 3.

[5] See Baqara 2:125; Hajj 22:26.

[6] Muslim, *Tahara,* 1.

[7] Tirmidhi, *Adab,* 41.

[8] Muslim, *Tahara,* 1; Tirmidhi, *Da'awat,* 91; Nasai, *Zakat,* 1.

[9] Muslim, *Tahara,* 1; Tirmidhi, *Da'awat,* 91; Nasai, *Zakat,* 1.

[10] Akademi Araştırma Heyeti, *Bir Müslümanın Yol Haritası,* 239-240.

[11] Imam Ghazzali, *Ihya Ulum al-Din,* 1:374-5.

[12] http://www2.kenyon.edu/Depts/Religion/Projects/Reln91/Blood/Judaism/new%20family/purity.htm

[13] http://www.cirp.org/library/cultural/councilflorence

[14] Sahih Muslim, *Kitab al-Qadr* (The Book of Destiny), Hadith 6423.

[15] M. Fethullah Gülen, *İnancın Gölgesinde,* 1:252.

[16] Tirmidhi, *Adab* 41.

[17] Muslim, *Tahara* 1; Tirmidhi, *Daawat* 86; Ahmad Ibn Hanbal, *Musnad,* 4:260, 5:342, 343, 344, 363, 370, 372; Darimi, *Wudu* 2.

[18] Muslim, *Jum'a* 9.

[19] Muslim, *Tahara* 20-21.

[20] Abu Dawud, *Tahara* 27, 30; Muslim, *Tahara* 45; Nasai, *Tahara* 8.

[21] Nasai, *Tahara* 5.

[22] Bukhari, *Wudu* 26; Muslim, *Tahara* 87; Muwatta, *Tahara* 9; Abu Dawud, *Tahara* 49; Tirmidhi, *Tahara* 19; Nasai, *Tahara* 1.

[23] Tirmidhi, *Tahara* 40.

[24] M. Fethullah Gülen, *İnancın Gölgesinde,* I, 17.

[25] Mehmet Dikmen, *Cep Ilmihali.*

[26] Bukhari, *Iman,* 29.

[27] Ibn Maja, *Tahara,* 9.

[28] Ibn Maja, *Tahara,* 10, 40.

[29] M. Fethullah Gülen, *İnancın Gölgesinde,* I, 179.

30 An expert who studies epidemics, the way they spread and their treatments

31 An expert who studies bacteria

32 Ailments that are related to or caused by the antibodies of the immune system

33 Cesur, Ibrahim, *Sızıntı Dergisi*, Issue: 262, November 2000.

CHAPTER 2
THINGS THAT ARE CLEAN AND THOSE THAT ARE NOT IN ISLAM

1 A white sticky fluid that flows from the sexual organs when thinking about sexual intercourse, during foreplay, and so on.

2 A thick white cloudy secretion, which has no smell, discharged after urination and ccasionally before.

3 Akademi Araştırma Heyeti, *Bir Muslumanın Yol Haritası*, 307.

4 Akademi Araştırma Heyeti, *Bir Müslümanın Yol Haritası*, 309.

5 Vehbe Zuhayli, *Islam Fıkhı Ansiklopedisi*, 6/149.

6 Dikmen, Mehmet, *Cep İlmihali*.

7 Abu Dawud, *Tahara*, 41; Nasai, *Tahara*, 46; Tirmidhi, *Tahara*, 52.

8 Abu Dawud, *Sunan*, 3809.

9 Al-Mawsili, *Al-Ikhtiyar*, 5:13.

10 Bukhari, *Mishkat al-Masabih*, 3:1392.

11 Bukhari, *Shurb*, 9; *Adab*, 27; Muslim, *Salaam*, 153.

12 Muslim, *Al-Birr was-Salat*, 60; Tirmidhi, *Qiyama*, 2; Ahmad ibn Hanbal, *Musnad*, 2:235, 323, 363, 30, 441.

13 Bukhari, *Sahih Bukhari*, 3:322.

14 Haysami, *Majma al-Zawaid*, 8:196

15 Bukhari, *Zabaih*, 6; Muslim, *Musaqat*, 46, 50, 56-58; Abu Dawud, *Tahara*, 89; Bukhari, *Bad al-Halk*, 7, 17; *al-Libas*, 77; Muslim, *Libas*, 81.

16 http://www.religionlink.org/tip_030903b.php

17 Muslim, Ahmad, Abu Dawud, and al-Bayhaqi.

18 Ibn Maja, *Libas*, 25.

19 Tirmidhi, *Libas*, 1.

20 The issue of absolute and conditional water will be further explained in the following chapters.

21 Ibn Maja, *Libas*, 25.

22 Hakim al-Nisaburi, *Al-Mustadrak*, 1/293.

23 Ibn Abidin, *Hashiyah al-Radd al-Muhtar*, 1/344.

CHAPTER 3
PHYSICAL CLEANLINESS

[1] Aslan Mayda, *"Çevre Temizliği,"* Sızıntı Dergisi, Aralık 2002, Year: 24, Issue: 287.

[2] Mesut Mutlu, *"Beden Temizliği,"* Sızıntı Degisi, Mayıs 2003, Year: 25, Issue: 292.

[3] Suyuti, *Jami al-Saghir*, 2, 72.

[4] Daylami, *Firdaws*, 3:205.

[5] Muslim, *Tahara*, 56; Abu Dawud, *Tahara* 29; Tirmidhi, *Adab* 14; Nasai, *Ziynat* 1.

[6] Abu Davud, *Tahara* 55.

[7] Muslim, *Tahara* 20, 21.

[8] Bukhari, *Jum'a*, 8; Muslim, *Tahara*, 42.

[9] Bukhari, *Sawm*, 27.

[10] Abu Dawud, *Tahara*, 27, 30; Muslim, *Tahara*, 45; Nasai, *Tahara*, 8.

[11] Ibn Maja, *Tahara*, 7; Bukhari, *Jum'a*, 8, *Tamanni*, 9; Muslim, *Tahara*, 42; Muwatta, *Tahara*, 115; Abu Dawud, *Tahara*, 115; Tirmidhi, *Tahara*, 18; Nasai, *Tahara*, 5, 7.

[12] Bukhari, *Sawm*, 27; Nasai, *Tahara*, 4; Ibn Maja, *Tahara*, 7; Darimi, *Wudu* 19.

[13] Muslim, *Iman*, 147; Ibn Maja, *Dua*, 10.

[14] Hydrotherapy is the treatment of diseases with water.

[15] See the Qur'an, 5:6.

[16] Wahba Zuhayli, *Encyclopedia of Islamic Jurisprudence*, 3/544.

[17] Abu Dawud, *Tarajjul*, 3.

[18] Abu Dawud, *Tarajjul*, 14.

[19] Bukhari, *Libas*, 72; Muslim, *Libas*, 72; Abu Dawud, *Tarajjul*, 14; Nasai, *Ziynat*, 5; Ibn Maja, *Libas*, 38; Ahmad ibn Hanbal, *Musnad*, 2:39. This hadith was also reported by Abu Hanifa. See Zabidi, *Uqud al-Jawahir al-Munifa*, 2:156.

[20] Abu Dawud, *Tarajjul*, 13; Nasai, *Ziynat* 57; Ahmad ibn Hanbal, *Musnad*, 1:204.

[21] Abu Dawud, *Libas*, 4; Ahmad ibn Hanbal, *Musnad*, 2:50.

[22] Hakim al-Nisaburi, *Mustadrak*, 4:150.

[23] M. Fethullah Gülen, *Prizma IV*, 119-123.

[24] Muslim, *Tahara*, 87.

[25] Muslim, *Tahara*, 56; Tirmidhi, *Adab*, 14.

[26] Ibn Maja, *Tahara*, 28.

[27] Ibn Maja, *Tahara*, 28.

[28] Mesut Mutlu, *"Beden Temizliği,"* Sızıntı Dergisi, Mayıs 2003, Year: 25, Issue: 292.

[29] Aslan Mayda, *"Çevre Temizliği,"* Sızıntı Dergisi, Aralık 2002, Year: 34, Issue: 287.

[30] Tabarani, *Al-Mujam al-Kabir*, 18:225.

[31] Mawsili, *Ikhtiyar*, 1/35-36.
[32] Mawsili, *Ikhtiyar*, 1/35-36.
[33] Wahba Zuhayli, *Encyclopedia of Islamic Jurisprudence*, 1/127.
[34] Muslim, *Ashriba*, 96-99; see also Bukhari, *Ashriba*, 22, *Bad al-Khalq*, 11, 14; *Isti'zan* 49, 50; Abu Dawud, *Ashriba,* 22.
[35] Aslan Mayda, "*Çevre Temizliği*," Sızıntı Dergisi, Aralık 2002, Year: 24, Issue: 287.
[36] An'am 6:121.
[37] Abu Dawud, *Adahi*, 15; Ibn Maja, *Zabaih,* 5; Ahmad ibn Hanbal, *Musnad*, 4:256.
[38] Bukhari, *Zabaih*, 15-18, 23; Muslim, *Adahi*, 22.
[39] Bukhari, *Sharika*, 3; Muslim, *Adahi*, 20.
[40] Qaradawi, *Al-Halal wal-Haram fil Islam*, 52-53.
[41] See Maeda 5:5.
[42] Ahmed Şahin, *Zaman Gazetesi*, 08.06.2005
[43] Ahmad ibn Hanbal, *Musnad*, 5:335, Tabarani, *Mu'jam al-Kabir*, 6:131.
[44] Ibrahim Canan, *Islam'da Çevre Sağlığı* (Environmental Issues of Health in Islam), 68-69.
[45] Haysami, *Majma al-Zawaid*, 1:104.
[46] M. Yusuf Kandahlawi, *Hayat al-Sahaba*, 3:77.
[47] Ibn Maja, *Masajid*, 4.
[48] Ahmad ibn Hanbal, *Musnad*, 3:407-8.
[49] Abu Dawud, *Salat*, 13; Tirmidhi, *Salat*, 412.
[50] Ibn Maja, *Masajid*, 4.
[51] Aslan Mayda, "*Çevre Temizliği*," Sızıntı Dergisi, Aralık 2002, Year: 24, Issue: 287.
[52] Ahmad ibn Hanbal, *Musnad*, 2:259, 265.
[53] M. Yusuf Kandahlawi, *Hayat al-Sahaba*, 3:77.
[54] Ibn Asir, *Usd al-Ghaba*, 7:391.
[55] Haysami, *Majma al-Zawaid*, 8:258; Bayhaqi, *Sunan*, 1/212.
[56] Haysami, *Majma al-Zawaid*, 2:11.
[57] Ibn Qayyim, *al-Tib al-Nabawi*, p. 216.
[58] Muslim, *Tahara*, 68.
[59] Haysami, *Majma al-Zawaid*, 1:204.
[60] Azimabadi, *Tuhfat al-Ahwazi*, 1:48; Sindi, *Hashiya ala ibn Maja*, 1:138-9.
[61] İbrahim Canan, *Ayet ve Hadislerin Işığında Çevre Ahlakı*, 87-89.
[62] Muslim, *Iman*, 58; Bukhari, *Hiba*, 35; Abu Dawud, *Adab*, 160; Tirmidhi, *Iman*, 6; Nasai, *Iman*, 16; Ibn Maja, *Adab*, 9.
[63] Muslim, *Zakat*, 55; Bukhari, *Mazalim*, 24; Abu Dawud, *Tatawwu*, 12.

64 Muslim, *Birr*, 128-130; Ibn Maja, *Adab*, 7; Ahmad ibn Hanbal, *Musnad*, 2:304, 343, 416.

65 Ibn Maja, *Adab*, 7.

66 Muslim, *Birr*, 131, 132.

67 *Mujam al-Wasit*, 1:12.

68 Ibn Asir, *Al-Nihaya*, 1:34.

69 İbrahim Canan, *Ayet ve Hadislerin Işığında Çevre Ahlakı*, 89-90.

70 *United Nations Water Conference*, 1977.

71 Aslan Mayda, "Çevre Temizliği," Sızıntı Dergisi, December 2002, Year: 24, Issue: 287.

72 Mursalat 77:1-2.

73 Dhariyat 51:1.

74 Ibn Haldun, *Muqaddima*, 347-8.

75 For further information see: İbrahim Canan, *Ayet ve Hadislerin Işığında Çevre Ahlakı*, 106-8.

CHAPTER 4
RITUAL PURIFICATION

1 See Baqara 2:222.

2 Muslim, *Tahara*, 32; Muwatta, *Tahara*, 31; Tirmidhi, *Tahara*, 2.

3 Ahmad ibn Hanbal, *Musnad*, 1:307; Hakim, *Mustadrak*, 3:623.

4 Muslim, *Dhikr*, 41; Abu Dawud, *Salat*, 361.

5 Tirmidhi, *Qadar*, 7; Ibn Maja, *Muqaddima*, 13.

6 M. Fethullah Gülen, *Asrın Getirdiği Tereddütler*, 4:236.

7 Bukhari, *Mawaqit* 6; Muslim, *Masajid* 282; Tirmidhi, *Amsal*, 5; Nasai, *Salat*, 7; Muwatta, *Safar*, 91.

8 Muslim, *Birr*, 33; Ibn Maja, *Zuhd*, 9.

9 Muslim, *Musafirin*, 294.

10 Bukhari, *Wudu*, 26; Muslim, *Tahara*, 87.

11 Muslim, *Tahara*, 41; Muwatta, *Safar*, 55; Tirmidhi, *Tahara*, 39; Nasai, *Tahara*, 106.

12 See: Muhammad Hamidullah, *İslam'a Giriş*, trans. Cemal Aydın, 86; Süleyman Uludağ, *İslam'da Emir ve Yasakların Hikmeti*, 76.

13 Hujwiri, *Kashf al-Mahjub*, trans. Süleyman Uludağ, 426, 428.

14 Ahmed Avni Konuk, *Tedbîrât-ı İlahiye Tercüme ve Şerhi* (Annotated translation of Ibn Arabi's *Tadbirat al-Ilahiya*), 1992, 431.

15 Abu Dawud, *Sunan, Adab*, 3; also see Mehmet Demirci, "İbadetlerin İç Anlamı," Tasavvuf Dergisi, Issue: 3, Ankara, 2000.

16 Bukhari, *Wudu*, 3; Muslim, *Tahara*, 34, 35, 40; Nasai, *Tahara*, 110.

[17] Muslim, *Tahara*, 65; Tirmidhi, *Tahara*, 41.

[18] Abu Dawud, *Tahara*, 65; Tirmidhi, *Tahara*, 41.

[19] Akademi Araştırma Heyeti, *Bir Müslümanın Yol Haritası*, 255.

[20] Wahba Zuhayli, *İslam Fıkıh Ansiklopedisi*, 1/614.

[21] Akademi Araştırma Heyeti, *Bir Müslümanın Yol Haritası*, 2005, 258-259.

[22] Muslim, *Tahara*, 41; Tirmidhi, *Tahara*, 39.

[23] Ahmad ibn Hanbal, *Musnad*, 4/226.

[24] Bukhari, *Wudu*, 35, 48; Muslim, *Tahara*, 72.

[25] Wahba Zuhayli, *İslam Fıkıh Ansiklopedisi*, 1/332-3.

[26] Akademi Araştırma Heyeti, *Bir Müslümanın Yol Haritası*, 262-67.

[27] For Sulami's (d. 1021) views concerning this issue, see Süleyman Ateş, *Sülemi ve Tasavvufi Tefsiri*, 143.

[28] Muhyiddin ibn Arabi, *Fusus al-Hikam*, quoted in Mehmet Demirci, *"İbadetlerin İç Anlamı"* (The Inner Meaning of Acts of Worship), Tasavvuf Dergisi, Issue:3, Ankara, 2000.

[29] Mehmet Demirci, *"İbadetlerin İç Anlamı"* (The Inner Meaning of Acts of Worship), Tasavvuf Dergisi, Issue:3, Ankara, 2000.

[30] Hafid ibn Rushd, *Bidayat al-Mujtahid*, 1/35.

[31] Bukhari, *Ghusl*, 26.

[32] Bukhari, *Ghusl*, 23.

[33] Bukhari, *Hayd*, 2.

[34] Akademi Araştırma Heyeti, *Bir Müslümanın Yol Haritası*, 268-272.

[35] Tabarani, *Mujam al-Awsat*, 1/90.

[36] See Baqara 2:222.

[37] Bukhari, *Hayd*, 20; Muslim, *Hayd*, 69.

[38] Haluk Nurbaki, *Diyanet Gazetesi*, Issue: 290, 14-15.

[39] Nasai, *Tahara*, 133, 134, 137; *Hayd*, 2, 4, 6; Darimi, *Wudu*, 84.

[40] Abu Dawud, *Tahara*, 110.

[41] Akademi Araştırma Heyeti, *Bir Müslümanın Yol Haritası*, 276–77.

CHAPTER 5
SPIRITUAL CLEANLINESS AND PURITY

[1] M. Fethullah Gülen, *Fasıldan Fasıla*, IV, 75.

[2] Bukhari and Muslim, *Sahih Bukhari*, II, 9.

[3] Ghazali, *Ihya al-Ulum al-Din*, (Revival of Religious Learnings).

[4] Al-Qushayri, *Al-Risala*, 327.

[5] M. Fethullah Gülen, *Sufism, Emerald Hills of the Heart*, 1/18-19.

[6] Bayhaqi, *Shuab al-Iman*, 5/441.

7   M. Fethullah Gülen, *Asrın Getirdiği Tereddütler*, 4/106–111.

8   Muhammed Emin Er, *Fıkh-ı Batın*, 15–22.

9   M. Yusuf Kandahlawi, *Hayat al-Sahaba*, 2/164.

10 Darimi, *Wudu*, 2; *Musnad*, V/342–344.

11 Munawi, *Fayd al-Qadir*, III/366; Ibn Maja, *Tijara*, 1.

12 Munawi, *Fayd al-Qadir*, III/367.

13 Munawi, *Fayd al-Qadir*, III/322.

14 Ibn Maja, *Zuhd*, 5.

15 Bukhari, *Buyu*, 15.

16 Mawsıli, *Al-Ikhtiyar*, 4/171–172.

17 Muslim, *Musaqat*, 106, 107, 113; Tirmidhi, *Buyu*, 2; Abu Dawud, *Buyu*, 4; Ibn Maja, *Tijara*, 58; Nasai, *Ziynat*, 25.

18 Tirmidhi, *Buyu*, 58; Ibn Maja, *Ashriba*, 6.

19 Muslim, *Iman*, 164; Tirmidhi, *Buyu*, 74; Abu Dawud, *Buyu*, 52; Ibn Maja, *Tijara*, 36.

20 Muslim, *Iman*, 164; Tirmidhi, *Buyu*, 74; Abu Dawud, *Buyu*, 52; Ibn Maja, *Tijara*, 36.

21 Muslim, *Musaqat* 129; Abu Dawud, *Buyu*, 49; Tirmidhi, *Buyu*, 40.

22 Ahmad ibn Hanbal, *Musnad*, 2/33.

23 Bediüzzaman Said Nursi, *Words*, 427–8.

24 Al-Nawawi, *Al-Nawawi's forty hadiths, Hadith no. 10*, see also Muslim, Tirmidhi, Ahmad.

25 Bukhari, *Buyu*, 50, *Tafsir*, *Fath* 3.

26 See, for instance, A'raf 7:26.

27 See Baqara 2:197.

28 See Baqara 2:222.

BIBLIOGRAPHY

Abu Dawud, *Al-Sunan*, Dar al-Jinan, Beirut, 1988.

Abu Nuaym, *Hilyah al-Awliya*, Dar al-Kitab al-'Arabi: Beirut, 1405 AH.

Ahmad ibn Hanbal, *Al-Musnad*, Beirut, 1969.

Ahmet Avni Konuk, *Tedbirat-ı İlahiye Tercüme ve Şerhi* (Annotated Interpretation of Muhyiddin ibn Arabi's *Tadbirat al-Ilahiyya*), Istanbul, 1992.

Ahmet Şahin, ahmetsahin.org, 08.11.2003; 05.15.2003;

—— Zaman Daily 08.06.2005.

Akademi Araştırma Heyeti, *Bir Müslümanın Yol Haritası*, Işık Yayınları: Izmir, 2005.

Al-Qaradawi, *Al-Halal wa'l-Haram fi'l-Islam*, Beirut, 1967.

Ali al-Muttaqi, *Kanz al-'Ummal fi Sunan al-Aqwal wal-Af'al*, Muassasa al-Risala: Beirut, 1989.

Aslan Mayda, "*Çevre Temizliği*," Sızıntı, December 2002, Issue: 287.

'Azimabadi, *Tuhfat al-Ahwazi*, Beirut, undated.

Bayhaqi, *Al-Sunan al-Kubra*, Dairah al-Maarif al-Uthmaniyya: Haydarabad, 1344 AH.

Bazzar, *Musnad*, Muassah al-'Ulum al-Qur'an: Beirut, 1410 AH.

Bediüzzaman Said Nursi, *Risale-i Nur Külliyatı*, Nesil Yayınları: Istanbul, 2002.

Bukhari, *Al-Jami al-Sahih*, Dar al-Kutub al-'Ilmiyya, Beirut:1994.

Darimi, *Sunan al-Darimi*, Dar al-Kitab al-'Arabi, Beirut, 1987.

Daylami, *Firdaws*, Dar-al Kutub al-'Ilmiyya: Beirut, 1986.

Elmalılı Hamdi Yazır, *Hak Dini Kur'an Dili*, Eser Neşriyat: Istanbul, 1978.

Ghazali, *Ihya al-Ulum al-Din*, Arslan Yayınları: Istanbul, 1993.

Hakim al-Nisaburi, *Al-Mustadrak al-Sahihayn*, Dar al-Kutub al-'Ilmiyya, Beirut, 1990.

Haluk Nurbaki, Diyanet Gazetesi, Issue 290;

—— *Kur'an-ı Kerim'den Ayetler ve İlmi Gerçekler*, Türkiye Diyanet Vakfı: Ankara, 1993.

Haysami, *Majma al-Zawaid wa Manba' al-Fawaid*, Dar al-Kitab al-'Arabi, Beirut, 1987.

Heyet, *Mujam al-Wasit*, Çağrı Yayınları: Istanbul, undated.

Hujwiri, *Kashf al-Mahjub*, translated as Hakikat Bilgisi by Süleyman Uludağ, Istanbul, 1982.

Hüseyin Çelik, *Temizlik Doğudan Gelir*, Türkiye Diyanet Vakfı Yayınları: Ankara, 1995.

Ibn 'Abdilbarr, *Jami' al-Bayan al-'Ilm*, Dar al-Ibn al-Jawzi, Damam, 1994.

Ibn 'Abidin, *Hashiyah Rad al-Muhtar*, Sharika Maktab wa Matba'a Mustafa al-Babi al-Halabi: Cairo, 1966.

Ibn Asir, *Al-Nihaya*, Dar al-Ihya al-Kutub al-Arabiyya: Cairo1963;

—— *Usd al-Ghaba*, Dar al-Shaab: Cairo, 1970.

Ibn Hajar, *Fath al-Bari*, Dar al-Ma'rifa: Beirut, 1379 AH.

Ibn Haldun, *Mukaddime*, Milli Eğitim Gençlik ve Spor Bakanlığı: Ankara, 1988.

Ibn Kathir, *Tafsir al-Qur'an al-'Azim*, Kahraman Yayınları: Istanbul, 1984.

Ibn Maja, *Al-Sunan*, Dar al-Kutub al-Ilmiyya: Beirut, undated.

Ibn Manzur, *Lisan al-'Arab*, Beirut, undated.

Ibn Qayyim, *Al-Tib al-Nabawi*, Dar al-Ihya al-Turas al-Arabi, Beirut, 1957.

Ibn Rushd, *Bidayah al-Mujtahid*, Dar al-Kahraman, Istanbul, undated.

Ibn Sa'd, *Al-Tabaqat al-Kubra*, Beirut, 1985.

Jurjani, *Kitab al-Ta'rifat*, Istanbul, 1300 AH.

Imam Malik, *Al-Muwatta*, Dar al-Hadith: Cairo, 1993.

İbrahim Canan, *Ayet ve Hadislerin Işığında Çevre Ahlakı*, Yeni Asya Yayınları: Istanbul, 1995;

—— *İslam'da Çevre Sağlığı*, Istanbul, 1986.

İbrahim Cesur, "Ne Kadar Temizlik?", Sızıntı, November 2000, Issue 262.

M. Fethullah Gülen, *Asrın Getirdiği Tereddütler*, TÖV Yayınları: Izmir, 1992;

—— *Fasıldan Fasıla I-III*, Nil Yayınları: Istanbul, 1997;

—— *Fasıldan Fasıla IV*, Nil Yayınları: Istanbul, 2001;

—— *İktisat* (sermon transcription), 1979;

—— *İnancın Gölgesinde I*, Nil Yayınları: Izmir, 2002;

—— *Kırık Testi*, Gazeteciler ve Yazarlar Vakfı Yayınları: Istanbul, 2004;

—— *Pearls of Wisdom*, Light Inc.: NJ, 2006;

—— *Prizma II*, Nil Yayınları: Izmir, 2002;

—— *Prizma IV*, Nil Yayınları: Istanbul, 2003;

—— *Sufism, Emerald Hills of the Heart I-II*, Light Inc.: NJ, 2004.

M. Fuad 'Abdulbaqi, *Mu'jam al-Mufahras li Alfaz al-Qur'an*, Dar al-Hadith: Cairo, 1988.

M. Yusuf Kandahlawi, *Hayat al-Sahaba*, Divan Yayınları: Istanbul, 1990.

Mawsili, *Al-Ikhtiyar*, Çağrı Yayınları: Istanbul, 1987.

Mehmed Paksu, *Açıklamalı İslam İlmihali*, Yeni Asya Yayınları: Istanbul, 1990.

Mehmet Demirci, "*İbadetlerin İç Anlamı*," Tasavvuf Dergisi, Issue 3, Ankara, 2000.

Mehmet Dikmen, *Cep İlmihali*, Cihan Yayınları, Istanbul, undated.

Mesut Mutlu, "*Beden Temizliği*," Sızıntı, May 2003, Issue: 292.

Muhammed Emin Er, *Fıkh-ı Batın*, Arş Sanat Yayınevi: Istanbul, 2003.

Muhammad Hamidullah, *İslam'a Giriş*, trns. Cemal Aydın, Ankara, 1996.

Munawi, Fayd al-Qadir, *Dar al-Kutub al-'Ilmiyya*, Beirut, 1994.

Muslim, *Sahih Muslim*, Dar al-Ihya al-Turath al-'Arabi: Beirut, undated.

Mustafa Tatçı (ed.), *Yunus Emre Divanı*, Ankara, 1991.

Nasai, *Al-Sunan al-Kubra*, Beirut, 1991.

Sindi, *Hashiya 'ala ibn Maja*, Maktabat al-Matbu'at al-Islamiyya, Aleppo, 1986.

Suyuti, *Jami al-Saghir*, Dar al-Tair al-'Ilm: Jiddah, undated.

Süleyman Ateş, *Sülemi ve Tasavvufi Tefsiri*, Istanbul, 1969.

Tabarani, *Mu'jam al-Kabir*, Maktabat al-'Ulum wa'l Hikam, Musul, 1983.

—— *Mu'jam al-Awsad*, Al-Maktab al-Islami: Beirut, 1985.

Tahanawi, *I'la al-Sunan*, Idarat al-Qur'an Wa'l Ulum: Karachi, 1415 AH.

Tirmidhi, *Al-Jami al-Sahih*, Beirut, undated.

Wahba Zuhayli, *İslam Fıkhı Ansiklopedisi* (trns.), Risale Yayınları: Istanbul, 1994.

Zabidi, *'Uqud al-Jawahir al-Munifa*, Beirut, undated.

Zamakhshari, *Atwaq al-Zahab*, Bedir Yayınları: Istanbul, 1994.

Zaylai, *Nasb al-Rayah*, Dar al-Hadith: Cairo, 1357 AH.

INDEX

A

ablution (*wudu'*), 16, 86, 99, 109, 116, 117, 121; ranks of, 95; types of, 105; of the excused, 106
'*ala al-makarih*, 90
apprehension, 8, 20, 23, 46
asbigh, 90

B

baptism, 10, 11

C

childbirth bleeding, 85, 109, 110, 111, 115, 123, 124, 125, 126, 127
Christianity, 10, 11
cleanliness of income and earnings, 138; interest, 140, 142, 143, 144, 147, 149; gambling, 144, 149; trading in intoxicants, 140, 144, 149; treachery in dealings and transactions, 145; profiteering, 146, 149; usury, 140, 146, 147, 149

D

Divine Names (Beautiful Names of God); *(Al-) Quddus* (Holiest, the; Purest, the), 17, 18; *(Al-) Latif* (All-Subtle, the), 54; *(Al-)* *Hakim* (All-Wise, the), 68; *(Al-) Ghaffar* (All-Forgiving, the) 95
dry ablution (*tayammum*), viii, 90, 102, 116, 117, 118, 119

E

elimination of annoyance, 79, 80

F

filth, actual or ritual (*najasa*) 27; heavy filth (*najasa al-ghaliza*), 27, 28, 30; light filth (*najasa al-khafifa*), 27, 28, 29, 32
fitrat (inborn natural predisposition), 12, 13, 53, 60

G

ghusl (complete ritual bath), 4, 15, 28, 33, 38, 46, 51, 56, 57, 61, 77, 85, 86, 93, 99, 101, 104, 105, 109, 117, 121, 158

H

halal (lawful, permitted) 69, 70, 71, 72, 73, 74, 138, 149, 156, 161
haram (unlawful), 30, 37, 55, 68, 70, 73, 74, 115, 116, 149, 156, 161
Hindu beliefs, 9

I

ibada, muthba (established acts of worship), 68; *manfi* (protective acts of worship), 68
immune system, 21, 22, 154
istibra, 18, 19, 44
istinja (cleaning the private parts), 44, 45, 46, 61

J

Judaism, 9, 10, 153

M

marine animals, 33
masiwa, 7
menstruation, 10, 62, 85, 86, 109, 110, 111, 121, 122, 123, 124, 125, 126
misogi, 9
miswak, 53, 54, 55, 100, 103

N

najis (impure), 27, 34, 37, 64, 71, 126
nazafat, 3, 17
niddah, 10
non-menstrual vaginal bleeding, vii, 28, 122, 124

P

pets, 33, 34, 35
pig bristle, 37
pure heart (*qalb al-saleem*), 18, 131, 132, 133

R

ritual impurity (*hadath*), viii, 10, 16, 61, 85, 86, 108, 109, 110, 111, 112, 115, 116, 117, 125, 126, 127, 128; minor impurity, 85; major impurity, 85

S

Shinto, 9
Sunna al-mu'akkada (confirmed practice of the Prophet), 15
Sunnatullah (God's Law), 17

T

tahara min najasa, 16; *tahara min hadath*, 16
tanning, 37, 43
thuhur, 6

V

vessels and utensils, 73

W

water; absolute, pure water; 47, 48; conditional water, 39, 47, 48, 154
wiping (*masah*), ix, 5, 17, 41, 92, 94, 99, 100, 101, 107, 108, 109, 117; indoor boots, 99, 102, 107, 108

Z

zarafat, 3